CULTURE SMART!
SPAIN

Marian Meaney

·K·U·P·E·R·A·R·D·

First published in Great Britain 2003
by Kuperard, an imprint of Bravo Ltd
59 Hutton Grove, London N12 8DS
Tel: +44 (0) 20 8446 2440 Fax: +44 (0) 20 8446 2441
www.culturesmartguides.com
Inquiries: sales@kuperard.co.uk

Culture Smart!® is a registered trademark of Bravo Ltd

Distributed in the United States and Canada
by Random House Distribution Services
1745 Broadway, New York, NY 10019
Tel: +1 (212) 572-2844 Fax: +1 (212) 572-4961
Inquiries: csorders@randomhouse.com

Revised 2008; sixth printing 2010

Series Editor Geoffrey Chesler

ISBN 978 1 85733 315 2

British Library Cataloguing in Publication Data
A CIP catalogue entry for this book is available from the
British Library

Printed in Malaysia

This book is available for special discounts for bulk purchases
for sales promotions or premiums. Special editions, including
personalized covers, excerpts of existing books, and corporate
imprints, can be created in large quantities for special needs.

For more information in the USA write to Special
Markets/Premium Sales, 1745 Broadway, MD 6–2, New York,
NY 10019, or e-mail specialmarkets@randomhouse.com.

In the United Kingdom contact Kuperard publishers at the
address at the top of the page.

About the Author

MARIAN MEANEY is a teacher, translator, and interpreter who has lived and worked in Spain for twenty years. After graduating with honors in English and Spanish from University College, Galway, she completed a higher diploma in Education, and was awarded a scholarship to study Spanish culture at the University of Salamanca. She subsequently ran English-language academies in Malaga and Barcelona, and has advised both Spanish businesses and government organizations on international exchange programs.

The Culture Smart! series is continuing to expand.
For further information and latest titles visit
www.culturesmartguides.com

The publishers would like to thank **CultureSmart!**Consulting for its help in researching and developing the concept for this series.

CultureSmart!Consulting creates tailor-made seminars and consultancy programs to meet a wide range of corporate, public-sector, and individual needs. Whether delivering courses on multicultural team building in the USA, preparing Chinese engineers for a posting in Europe, training call-center staff in India, or raising the awareness of police forces to the needs of diverse ethnic communities, it provides essential, practical, and powerful skills worldwide to an increasingly international workforce.

For details, visit www.culturesmartconsulting.com

CultureSmart!Consulting and **CultureSmart!** guides have both contributed to and featured regularly in the weekly travel program "Fast Track" on BBC World TV.

contents

contents

Map of Spain

introduction

In the popular imagination, Spain conjures up a picture of rapacious *conquistadores*, the unworldly Don Quixote, brave bullfighters, fiery flamenco dancers, and brilliant artists, from Goya and Velasquez to Picasso and Dali. All true enough—but how does the real, everyday Spain conform to these stereotypes?

The Spaniards are certainly distinctive. Visitors to Spain are astounded by their vitality, entranced by their friendliness, and driven mad by their relaxed attitude to deadlines. The Spanish people are proud, passionate, spontaneous, generous, and loyal; they can also be procrastinators, individualistic to a fault, suspicious, and noisy.

Spain has had a strong impact on European and world history. For almost seven hundred years under Moorish rule, Christians, Jews, and Muslims lived in harmony in Spain. Side by side, scholars from the different communities translated Greek and Roman texts, bringing the learning of classical antiquity to medieval Europe. Ironically, however, Spain did not benefit fully from the "new learning." In the wake of the Christian "reconquest" of 1492, Spain saw itself as the defender of the Catholic faith, and the Spanish Inquisition ended religious tolerance.

This, then, is the nation that enjoyed a golden age of enlightenment, that discovered America and gathered in its riches, and that left the great legacy of its culture and its language, which is today spoken by over three hundred million people. In the twentieth century, Spain suffered a bitter civil war and a stultifying dictatorship, and is now emerging from the isolation of the Franco regime to become once again an integral part of Europe and the international arena.

Culture Smart! Spain explores the complex human realities of modern Spanish life. It describes how Spain's history and geography have created both regional differences and shared values and attitudes. It reveals what the Spaniards are like at home, and in business, and how they socialize. The chapter on customs and traditions will prepare you, the visitor, for their boundless energy and religious devotion; the chapters on making friends and communicating are there to help you make the very most of your visit. The better you understand the Spanish people, the more you will be enriched by your experience of this vital, warm, and varied country—where the individual is important, and the enjoyment of life is paramount.

Key Facts

Official Name	Reino de España (Kingdom of Spain)	Member of NATO and European Union
Capital City	Madrid	
Main Cities	Barcelona, Valencia, Seville, Saragossa	
Area	194,899 sq. miles (504,788 sq. km)	
Geography	Spain covers four-fifths of the Iberian Peninsula; it is bordered by Portugal on the western side.	Spain is divided from France by the Pyrenees on the northeastern side.
Terrain	A great diversity of landscapes, including Mediterranean and Atlantic coastlines, a large central plateau, the *Meseta*, and several mountainous regions. The many rivers generally run east-west.	The main mountain ranges are the Pyrenees, the Cantabrian Mts. the Andalusian Mts. and the Sierra Nevada. The main rivers are the Tagus, the Ebro, and the Duero.
Climate	Mainly Mediterranean	Inland, Continental tendencies. In the north, temperate humid or maritime.
Currency	The euro, since January 1, 2002.	
Population	39,439,400 (est. 2000)	
Ethnic Makeup	Four major ethnic groups, divided by language.	Other ethnic minorities include *gitanos* (gypsies).

Language	Castilian (over 74%), Catalan (12%), Galician (8%), Basque (just over 1%).	
Religion	Roman Catholic 99%	
Government	Constitutional monarchy at the national level. The eighteen regions are autonomous communities.	The eighteen autonomous communities have the right to self-government under the Constitution.
Media	There are state and autonomous community television channels and private channels.	National newspapers with regional offices, including *El Pais*, *ABC*, *El Mundo*.
Media (English)	Various newspapers in different cities	
Electricity	220 volts, 50 Hz AC.	Two-prong plugs are used. Transformers needed for US appliances.
Video/TV	Pal B system	Some systems will play NTSC TV.
Telephone	Spain's country code is 34.	To dial out of Spain, dial 07.
Time	GMT + 1 hour; in summer, GMT + 2 hours	

chapter one

LAND &
PEOPLE

A GEOGRAPHICAL SNAPSHOT

One of the largest countries in Europe, Spain is situated on the Iberian Peninsula, which it shares with Portugal. The Pyrenees run across the neck of the peninsula and form Spain's border with France. The large central plateau, the *Meseta*, is bordered and divided by several mountain ranges. Madrid, situated at the geographical center, is the highest capital city in Europe.

Although Spain has rivers that are numbered among the longest in Europe (the Tagus, Ebro, and Duero), large areas of the country suffer from a scarcity of water. Linked to this problem is erosion, with millions of tons of topsoil being blown away each year. However, not all of Spain is dry or barren. The deep inlets of Galicia, the market gardens of Valencia, and the snowy highlands of the Pyrenees are just a few examples of Spain's variety of landscape.

From a tourist's point of view, the coastline is immensely important. Spain has over two thousand beaches, many of them of great beauty.

They are grouped together under famous names, such as the Costa Brava, Costa Dorada, Costa de Azahar, Costa Blanca, Mar Menor, Costa del Sol, Costa de la Luz, Rias Bajas and Rias Altas, Costa Cantábrica, Costa Canaria, and Costa Balear.

The total area of national territory is 194,897 square miles (504,788 sq. km), which includes the Canary and Balearic Islands and the two small enclaves of Ceuta and Melilla in Northern Africa. There is an incredible natural diversity to be enjoyed. As the British naturalists Chapman and Buck commented in their book *Wild Spain* (1893): "In no other land can there be found, within a similar area, such extremes of scene and climate."

CLIMATE

Although Spain lies in the temperate zone, its mountainous nature means that there are two differing climates: generally, wet and dry. The wet climate occurs in two main areas: the narrow coastal strip north of the Cantabrian mountains (the Basque Country, Cantabria, Asturias, and Galicia), and the northeastern coastal area from the French border down to Valencia, including the Balearic Islands. The former area shows only slight variations in temperature, with mild winters and cool summers. A cloudy sky and frequent rainfall are common, although less so during the summer. The latter area is hotter in the summer and has less rainfall.

The dry area occupies about two-thirds of the country and, although there are variations from one place to another, winters are cool (becoming extremely cold inland), with little rain. Summer brings a blazing sun in an intensely blue sky, with occasional, short-lived, local thunderstorms. The Canary Islands have a subtropical, Atlantic climate with an almost constant temperature of just over 68F° (20°C), with only minor variations between seasons.

REGIONAL POINTS OF VIEW

A Spaniard's first loyalty is to his region, not to Spain. His view of Spanish history depends on where he comes from, and how it influenced his particular region. There is, of course, no such thing as a typical Spaniard, but it is possible to distinguish people from different regions: the logical Catalans of the northeast, the hot-blooded Andalusians of the south, and the more serious Castilians of the central *Meseta*. In the past, mountain ranges hindered communications, different climates influenced local character, and divisions arose that still have not been overcome. Long before the Catholic monarchs Ferdinand and Isabella united the kingdoms of Castile and Aragon and unified Spain in 1492, there were various kingdoms within the peninsula, and Castilian dominance, for them, meant only a reduction in power. Spain was united in name only. The Golden Age did indeed bring great riches to the country, but not to the whole country, for most of the wealth was channeled to Castile or remained in the ports. Catalonia, which had been a major trading power, was at first not even allowed to trade with America.

The Basque Country and Catalonia never felt part of Spain, and fought hard for the autonomy they finally received in 1978. Catalonia sees itself as more modern, more European, than the rest of the country, and Spain is considered almost as a separate entity.

Even today, a Spaniard who moves to a different region can feel like a foreigner in his own country. In general, however, the modern Spaniard is proud of his country. When Franco died in 1975 he left Spain weary of dictatorship and hungry for democracy and a place in the international community. Less than thirty years later, it is on an equal standing with other first-world countries, and is a member of both the European Union and NATO.

A BRIEF HISTORY

It is impossible to do justice in a few pages to Spain's rich and varied history. What follows is merely a brief synopsis.

Early Inhabitants

The Iberian Peninsula has been occupied for hundreds of thousands of years. Bones of several individuals found in the *Cueva Mayor* ("Main Cave" at Atapuerca, Burgos) come from Middle Pleistocene sediments that are at least 280,000 years old.

The most advanced people living on the peninsula in classical antiquity were known as the Iberians. They lived along the Mediterranean and Southern Atlantic coasts, and are now thought to be natives of the peninsula. The Celts lived mainly in the north and west except for the western Pyrenees, where the Basques lived.

The Greeks came to Spain, but had only two settlements, in the northeast. Many of the Greek artifacts found in Spain were actually passed on

by Phoenician middlemen. In the ninth century
BCE the Phoenicians founded their first settlement
at Cadiz, and were to have an important impact
on Iberian culture. They traded oil and wine for
silver, but also brought religious ideas, skilled
metalworking, and literacy to the people. This is
sometimes known as the "orientalizing" period of
Spanish prehistory. The number of colonies
diminished toward the end of the sixth century;
those remaining were closer to Carthage, the most
important of the Phoenicians' western
Mediterranean settlements. However, by 218 BCE
the Carthaginians, under Hannibal, had pushed
far up the peninsula and brought upon
themselves the wrath of the Roman Empire.

The Romans
The Romans arrived in the second century BCE to
destroy the power of the Carthaginians and make
Spain part of their empire. It took them two
hundred years to subdue the people. They
constructed roads, irrigation systems, and
engineering marvels, some impressive examples of
which—such as the aqueduct at Segovia, the
bridge over the Tagus at Alcántara, or the
amphitheater at Mérida—remain to this day.
Spain's language, religion, and laws stem from this
period. Some of the upper classes in the towns
and cities of Spain formed part of the elite of the

Roman Empire. They included the philosopher and writer Seneca, the poet Martial, and several members of the Roman Senate, including Trajan and Hadrian, who later became emperors.

The Visigoths arrived in the fifth century CE, but the last Ibero-Roman strongholds did not fall until the seventh century CE.

The Arab Influence

In the year 711, Moors from north Africa sailed across the mere eight miles that separated them from Spain and, within a few years, had pushed the Visigoths right back to the Cantabrian Mountains in the north of the country. They remained in Spain for over eight hundred years, a time of tolerance when Muslims, Christians, and Jews lived together in peace. Medieval Spain was

the only multiracial and multireligious country in Western Europe, and much of the development of Spanish civilization in religion, literature, art, and architecture during the later Middle Ages stemmed from this fact. Many of the beautiful buildings built by the Moors—such as Seville's Giralda Tower and Alcázar and the magical Alhambra of Granada—still enchant us today.

Different emirates rose and fell during this time. One example, the Caliphate of Córdoba, produced a brilliant civilization that lasted just over a hundred years before splitting into a number of rival princedoms. The court culture embraced fields as varied as historiography, calligraphy, poetry, music, botany, medicine, mathematics, astronomy, ivory carving, and metalwork. The Moors stayed in Spain until 1492, although by the second half of the thirteenth century their power had been limited to the stronghold of Granada.

The *Reconquista*

The divisions among the Moors paralleled those occurring in Christian Spain. The country was divided into different kingdoms, which were unwilling to unite forces until the second half of the fifteenth century.

Finally, Ferdinand of Aragon and Isabella of Castile united their kingdoms with their marriage, and led the *reconquista*, or "reconquest," the name given to the struggle to gain back the territory lost to the "nonbelievers."

Aided by the Inquisition, they destroyed Spain's tolerant society and forced religious conversions. The Moors were not the only victims. The Jews had served Christian Spain and its monarchs well, providing an active commercial class and an educated elite for many administrative posts. But, inevitably, their wealth and heterodoxy caused jealousy and hatred in a population that saw itself as the defender of Christianity against the infidel.

From the start of the Spanish Inquisition in 1478, attempts at conversion were made more forcibly, and included confiscation of property, and torture, which often led to death. Soon after the last Moorish city, Granada, was taken, in 1492, all Jews who refused to convert to Christianity were expelled.

During the Reformation, fear of heresy led the Church to oppose new ideas, making Spain retreat into centuries of intellectual poverty.

By 1609 the last of the Moors had left, and Spain was bereft of both agricultural and administrative expertise. However, some influence remained. Many Christians from other countries had also studied with the Moors. One example was the School of Translators founded in the twelfth century at Toledo, where Jewish, Christian, and Muslim scholars had worked side by side. The resulting translations into Latin brought this treasury of human knowledge and philosophy not only to Spain, but also to Italy and France, planting the seeds of the Renaissance.

The Golden Age

The conquest of Granada allowed Castile to concentrate major resources and effort on overseas exploration instead of on domestic conflicts. The support that Christopher Columbus received from Isabella was indicative of this new policy. In 1492 Columbus made his great discovery of America—the New World. Spain and Portugal divided the spoils between them, and almost all of South America, Central America, North America, and the Philippines were added to the Spanish possessions. In the sixteenth century, Spain was the most important power in the world, with a huge empire, fleets on every sea, and a brilliant cultural, artistic, and intellectual life. Gold and silver, the primary objectives of the *conquistadores*, flowed into Spain in fabulous quantities.

When Charles I (elected Holy Roman Emperor in 1519 as Charles V) came to the throne, Spain was still divided into separate kingdoms and principalities. However, by the time he abdicated in favor of his son, Philip II, in 1556, Spain was on its way to becoming a centralized and absolute monarchy, although Catalonia, Navarre, Aragon, Valencia, and the Basque Country were still allowed a considerable degree of autonomy. This shift of power within Spain led to Catalonia, the most important trading region, not receiving any share in the new markets, and it was actually prohibited from dealing with the New World. By ridding itself of both the Jews and the Catalans, Spain deprived itself of its economically most active citizens and finally had to depend on German and Italian financiers.

Very little of the American treasure seems to have been invested in the economy. Most of it was used for display by the court, to pay for imports, for the armies abroad, and to satisfy foreign creditors. Thus Spain, with all the treasure of the New World at its command, remained a poor country.

During the sixteenth century the Church enlarged its already dominant position in Spanish life, and the Spanish Inquisition reached its greatest power. At the same time the Counter Reformation sought to reclaim Protestant Europe for the Church and to raise the spiritual tone of the Catholic countries. The Jesuit order, founded by St. Ignatius Loyola, an ex-soldier, was a major force. Its missionaries went all over the world and succeeded in converting millions to Catholicism. The life of a Jesuit was one of immense risk, and thousands of priests were persecuted or killed on their mission of conversion. However, in some nations, such as India and China, the Jesuits were welcomed as men of wisdom and science.

Education was of utmost importance to the Jesuits. In nearly every major city in Europe they established schools and colleges, and for a hundred and fifty years they were leaders in European education. (Through their loyalty to papal policies, the Jesuits were later drawn into the struggle between the papacy and the Bourbon monarchies and in the middle of the eighteenth century they were expelled from many countries including Spain. In 1814 they were reestablished once more.)

It was also a truly "Golden Age" for Spanish arts and literature. The novel reached its highest level with Cervantes' *Don Quixote*, which has been compared to Shakespeare's *Hamlet* and Homer's *Iliad*. Written to mock the popular novels of chivalry that glorified the ideals of courtesy, constancy, bravery, and loyalty, it was also considered part of the picaresque tradition (describing the adventures of a *pícaro*, a wandering rogue). There was a profusion of great poets, such as Garcilaso de la Vega, San Juan de la Cruz, and Luis de Góngora. The theater benefited from the many plays of Lope de

Vega, Tirso de Molina, and Calderón de la Barca. Likewise, in the world of art Diego Velasquez, "El Greco" (Domenikos Theotokopoulos), Zurbarán, and Murillo were prominent artists of the time.

The Decline

With Spain, Philip II had also inherited Sicily, Naples, Sardinia, Milan, Franche-Comté, the Netherlands, and all the Spanish colonies. However, a series of long, costly wars and revolts, capped by the defeat by the English of the "Invincible Armada" in 1588, began the steady decline of Spanish power in Europe. The nineteenth century brought invasion by Napoleon, who put his brother on the throne and started the furious conflict that the Spanish called the War of Independence and the English the Peninsular War. Spain ousted France, but only with the help of the British and the Portuguese. Later came the revolt and independence of most of Spain's colonies. There were also three wars over the succession, the brief ousting of the monarchy, and the establishment of the First Republic (1873–74), when the idea of Spain as a federal state was considered. Finally, the Spanish-American War (1898) sealed its fate. Spain lost Cuba, Puerto Rico, and the Philippines to the United States, and the days of empire were over.

By the end of the nineteenth century there were deep divisions within Spanish society. The Socialist and Anarcho-Syndicalist parties began to gain a wide following among the lower classes, particularly in industrial Catalonia, rural Andalusia, and in the mining districts of Asturias. Strikes and uprisings, suppressed with great brutality, became common. The Church, which supported the landowners, aroused anticlerical feeling, which was often violent, among revolutionary, and even liberal, elements. Meanwhile, the military watched everything closely in its self-imposed role as the guardian of the core values of Spanish society.

The king's support of General Miguel Primo de Rivera's military dictatorship in 1923 led to public mistrust and an overwhelming republican majority in the elections of 1931, after Primo de Rivera's resignation in 1930. Alfonso XIII went into exile (April 14, 1931). The government introduced a range of reforms, including autonomy for the Basque Country and Catalonia, and restrictions on the power of the Church. The conservatives feared even more changes and grouped together for the elections in 1933. Meanwhile, internal divisions among the left began to show and they ran as separate parties. They lost. The right-wing government immediately began to reverse the reforms carried out since 1931.

The Civil War

The next elections, in 1936, were won by the Popular Front, a coalition of several left-wing parties, and the reforms were reinstated once again. The conservatives immediately began to plan resistance. Rumors of a military coup led the government to transfer several high-ranking military officers to remote postings, hoping to make communication more difficult. (Francisco Franco was sent to Morocco.) Despite their efforts the conservative military rebellion took place on July 18. The organizers expected a quick victory. Instead, the civilian population took up arms in support of the government. The insurgents, or Nationalists, who soon came under the leadership of General Francisco Franco, embraced most conservative groups, notably the monarchists, most of the army officers, the clericalists, the landowners and industrialists, and the Carlists (a right-wing political movement, opposed to liberal secularism and economic and political modernism).

The right-wing rebels realized they would now have to look for outside help, and appealed to the fascist dictatorships in Italy, Germany, and Portugal, who sent supplies and men. The navy remained loyal to the government, so Hitler's pilots began by transporting soldiers and equipment from Spanish Morocco. Their destruction the following April of the Basque city of Guernica shocked the world.

Despite almost universal support for the Republic among British intellectuals and widespread support among the working classes, the British conservative government preferred not to act. Not only did it fear a larger international fight, but it was also more in sympathy with the rebels' conservative policies than the government's. France sympathized with the government but, fearing its own army, felt in too weak a position to do more. After sending a score of planes they proposed a nonintervention policy that was maintained throughout the war (although Germany and Italy merely ignored it). The left-wing Loyalists received some meager support only from Russia and Mexico.

The 1936 Spanish election had already been considered a great victory for the working classes, so the military uprising was seen as an assault against working people's interests everywhere. The rapid intervention of foreign troops made the Civil War international and it became an example of the growing worldwide struggle between fascism and democracy. Foreign volunteers arrived to fight on both sides. Those who fought with the Loyalists were called the international brigades.

They came from a variety of left-wing groups but were nearly always led by Communists. This created problems with other Republican groups, such as the Workers' Party of Marxist Unification (POUM) and the Anarchists, who provoked several days of rioting and fighting in May 1937 in Barcelona. This internal dissension on the Left damaged their spirit and weakened their army.

Despite military inferiority and bloody internal divisions, the Loyalists made a remarkably determined stand, particularly in central Spain. By the beginning of 1938, however, the territory held by the Loyalists had shrunk drastically, and with the fall of Barcelona in January 1939 the war was almost over. Madrid surrendered in March and the Loyalist government and many thousands of refugees fled into France.

In total, about 3.3 percent of the Spanish population died during the war, with another 7.5 percent being injured. Available information suggests that there were about 500,000 deaths from all causes during the Spanish Civil War. The economic blockade of Republican-controlled areas caused malnutrition in the civilian population that is believed to have caused the deaths of around 25,000 people. After the war it is believed that Franco's government arranged the executions of 100,000 Republican prisoners, and it is estimated that another 35,000 later died in concentration camps.

Franco's Dictatorship

A dictatorship was set up under Franco that restored the favored position of the Church and returned its properties. The *Movimiento Nacional* (National Movement) became the only political party, encompassing all right-wing groups, and the leftist opposition was suppressed. The Cortes (Parliament) and Catalan and Basque autonomy were abolished—although the Cortes was reestablished in 1942. Although it gave aid to the Axis (Germany and Italy) during World War II, Spain did not actually take part in the fighting. However, the United Nations, refusing to recognize the constitutionality of the Franco regime, in 1946 urged its members to break diplomatic relations with Spain; this resolution was not rescinded until 1950. An agreement with the United States in 1953 provided for U.S. bases in Spain and for economic and military aid. Spain entered the United Nations in 1955.

Political unrest, partly over the problem of succession to the Franco regime, became increasingly evident in the 1950s, and at the start of the 1960s the Church, which had long been silent, began to voice some opposition to aspects of the dictatorship. In 1962 a series of strikes, beginning in the coalfields of Asturias, indicated widespread discontent. Student demonstrations also occurred. Basque separatism posed another serious problem for the regime. Their terrorist organization, ETA (*Euskadi ta Askatasuna*), fought against the regime. Its greatest success was the murder of Franco's Prime Minister Carrero Blanco in 1973. During this regime ETA enjoyed a lot of public support, but this changed once democracy had been restored.

A new organic law (constitution) was announced by Franco in 1966. It separated the post of head of government from chief of state, provided for direct election of about one-quarter of the members of the Cortes, gave married women the vote, made religious freedom a legal right, and ended government control of labor unions. The forming of new political parties was still discouraged. Press censorship was ended in 1966, but strong guidelines remained.

Economically, Spain progressed dramatically in the 1960s and early 1970s, stimulated in part by the liberal economic policies espoused by Opus Dei (a Roman Catholic lay order promoting Christian values and working to suppress liberalism and immorality—controversial among Catholics because of its secretive nature, emphasis on discipline, and conservatism and wealth). Growth was particularly pronounced in the tourist, automobile, and construction industries.

The Transition

In 1969 Franco named his successor, Juan Carlos, the son of the legitimate heir to the throne, the king-in-exile Alfonso XIII. Juan Carlos had sworn an oath of allegiance to Franco and his regime and seemed to be willing to maintain it. In fact, he held reformist aspirations. The death of Franco on November 20, 1975, and the accession of Juan Carlos as king two days later, opened a new era: the peaceful transition to democracy. Arias Navarro, the conservative head of the government, was incapable of making the democratic transition that the king supported. When he resigned in 1976, Adolfo Suárez Gonzalez, a former Francoist minister, replaced him. Suárez entered office promising that elections would be held within one year, and his government moved to enact a series of laws to liberalize the new regime. Spain's first elections since 1936 were held on June 15, 1977. Suárez and his new party *Unión de Centro Democrático* (UCD) were returned with 34 percent of the vote. Under Suárez, the new Parliament set about drafting a democratic constitution that was overwhelmingly approved by voters in a national referendum in December 1978. Varying levels of autonomy were granted to the Basque Country, Catalonia, and the other regions in Spain. However, this was not enough for some of the

Basque separatists. ETA has continued to commit murders, although the violence has abated since the 1990s, when many leaders were arrested. Confronted by terrorism and economic recession, the UCD disintegrated into factions and, after heavy defeats in local elections, Suárez resigned in January 1981.

The inauguration of Leopoldo Calvo Sotelo, also a member of the UCD, was interrupted by the attempted military coup of Lieutenant Colonel Antonio Tejero, who occupied the Cortes (February 23, 1981) and held the government and the deputies for eighteen hours. It failed, owing to King Juan Carlos' resolute support of the democratic constitution. This was a turning point as the population accepted the king as a true champion of democracy, not a pawn of the old regime. Calvo Sotelo was left with the task of restoring confidence in democracy. His most notable achievement was Spain's entry into NATO in 1982.

The election of October 1982 marked the final break with the Francoist legacy by returning the *Partido Socialista Obrero Español* (PSOE) under its leader, Felipe González, with a solid majority to the Cortes. This was the first government in which none of the members had served under Francoism, and it paved the way toward a new future. Spain became a member of the European

Community in 1986 and in 1992 the country achieved prominence with the Expo '92 World's Fair in Seville and the Olympic Games in Barcelona. PSOE remained in power until 1996, when a center-right government took office. José María Aznar López, leader of the *Partido Popular* (PP) became prime minister in coalition with the Catalan nationalists. Aznar introduced a government austerity and privatization program, and the economy experienced significant economic growth. In 1999, Spain became part of the European Union's single currency plan and, benefiting from the prosperous economy, Aznar led the PP to a parliamentary majority in the March 2000 elections. Spain has finally become a stable democracy.

THE REGIONS

"The Iberians never would amalgamate, never would . . . put their shields together—never would sacrifice their own local private interest for the general good," said the nineteenth-century English traveler and writer Richard Ford. The Spanish are an individualistic race. A Spaniard's loyalty is to his village or town first, then to his region, and finally, if at all, to his country. This pride in their own region and a suspicion of outsiders' interference led to the division of Spain. Today it is divided into eighteen regions, or *comunidades autónomas* (autonomous communities): the Basque Country, Catalonia, Galicia, Andalusia, Asturias, Aragon, Balearic Islands, Canary Islands, Cantabria, Castile-León, Castile-La Mancha, Extremadura, Madrid, Murcia, Navarre, La Rioja, Valencia, and Ceuta and Melilla in North Africa.

For the first five years the central government allowed all regions control of the organization of institutions, urban planning, public works, housing, environmental protection, cultural affairs, sports and leisure, tourism, health and social welfare, and the cultivation of the regional language, where there was one. After five years they could accede to "full autonomy," but the meaning of this phrase was not clearly defined.

The transfer of powers to the autonomous governments has been determined in an ongoing process of negotiation between the individual communities and the central government. This process has given rise to repeated disputes. The communities, especially Catalonia, have complained that the central government has dragged its feet in ceding powers and in clarifying financial arrangements. Not all regions have the same powers. For instance, the Basque Country and Catalonia have their own police forces, and Navarre has a different financial arrangement from the others. Indeed, some regions deserve a special mention.

The "historic" regions—the Basque Country, Catalonia, and Galicia—should be considered separately. They are in the north of the country, nearer to France, and have a more moderate climate than most of Spain. They were under Moorish rule for only a short time, if at all. They have their own languages (not dialects) and traditions. Galicia is the poorest of the regions, and is not as vocal about autonomy as the others. The Basque Country and Catalonia are the most industrialized areas in Spain, and have a different work ethic from the rest of the country. They do not like to be referred to as Spanish, and show fierce loyalty to their own flags (the *ikurriña* in the Basque Country and the *senyera* in Catalonia). Andalusia is the largest region in Spain, visited by many thousands of tourists each year. It also deserves a special mention because it epitomizes traditional Spain.

The Basque Country (Euskal Herria)
The Basques occupied the northern part of Spain (and part of France) thousands of years before the

rise of the Roman Empire. Their region is known as *Euskal Herria*, or *Euskadi* in their own language, *Euskera*. This language is neither Latin-based nor related to any of the Indo-European languages, and there is much speculation about its roots. Researchers have linked it to languages in many other parts of the world, but none of these links can be proven.

As a race the Basque people are very different from their neighbors. They are taller and sturdier, and they have the highest proportion of rhesus-negative blood in Europe (25 percent), and one of the highest percentages of type O blood (55 percent). Fiercely independent, they retained their own sovereignty until nearly the fourteenth century. Even then they were only nominally integrated and could veto laws by saying "we obey but do not comply." It was not until the nineteenth century that the centralist government in Madrid deprived them of these rights. Fearing for their language and their culture, they began pressing for reforms and for greater autonomy. However, the Civil War and fascist dictatorship that followed prohibited all outward signs of Basque identity, and the very speaking of *Euskera* was declared illegal.

The Basques suffered terribly during the Spanish Civil War and under the subsequent oppression. They gradually began to organize themselves clandestinely, and the Basque separatists, ETA, have been fighting for independence since 1959. Although many of their members left once autonomy was achieved, some hard-core members remained. They have continued terrorist attacks throughout Spain, hoping to achieve complete independence for the Basque Country. However, they no longer have the support of the majority.

If you visit this region, you will find the scenery beautiful and the food wonderful. The people drink more than in other areas, and drunkenness is not as frowned upon. Spanish is still the dominant language, which is just as well, as you will not understand a word of *Euskera*. The Basques are a proud people, with a rich heritage that merits respect.

Catalonia (Catalunya)

Catalonia is situated on the northwestern Mediterranean coast, close to the French border. It has a population of six million, with 75 percent of this number living in or near the capital, Barcelona. Commercially successful, it is the richest region of Spain and considers itself more "European" than other areas. Catalan, the local language, stems from Latin but sounds very different from Spanish in that many two-syllable Latin words are reduced to one. For example, *noctem* (night) becomes *noche* in Spanish and *nit* in Catalan, and *totus* (all) is *todo* in Spanish and *tot* in Catalan.

Like the Basque Country, Catalonia has never felt itself to be part of Spain. Despite being subject to Castile and Aragon from 1479, it maintained its own local government until the eighteenth century and the Spanish War of Succession. It had its own Mediterranean empire at one stage, and today Catalan is still spoken in the town of Alguers in Sardinia.

On September 11, 1714, the Bourbon troops entered Barcelona. It was like 1066 to the English. The government was suppressed, Spanish became the language of administration, universities were closed, and Catalonia was totally under the control of Madrid. During Franco's dictatorship Catalan was not permitted in schools, and was only gradually allowed in public. When autonomy was granted reforms started. Now, Catalan is used as a daily language and the old institutions are back again.

There have been a large number of immigrants to Catalonia from the poorer regions of Spain. As the numbers grew (a million in the 1960s alone), Spanish language and customs began to take over. It was a culture shock for both sides. The Catalans expected their regional traditions to be accepted, while the newcomers could not see why they should be expected to change. After all, they were still in their own country.

The Catalan people have few of the characteristically Spanish traits. They are hardworking, conscientious, reliable, and serious. (Other Spaniards see them as mean, boring, and materialistic.) They are not as spendthrift, or generous, as the others (the term depending on your point of view). They do not buy rounds of drinks, but will pay for their own. They are not as friendly as the rest of the Spaniards, but this is due to a natural reserve on their part. They are polite and helpful, if asked, but will not intrude. Foreigners will have few problems here. Life is more similar to that in other parts of Europe, but you may miss the warm welcome of other parts of Spain.

Galicia

Galicia is the other region of Spain that has its own language and nationalistic feeling. It is situated in the cold, wet, northwest corner of the peninsula. It shares a similar climate and mastery of poetry, songs, and music with the Celtic countries (Ireland, Wales, and Scotland). Despite emphasizing its Celtic links, there is no evidence that this region had any more contact with the Celts than any other.

Unlike the Basque and Catalan regions, Galicia remains relatively poor, agricultural, and dominated by rural society. It is estimated that for the last five centuries one in three Galician males had to leave his homeland to work in another part of Spain, Europe, or South America. In some parts of South America the word *gallego* (meaning "Galician") is a synonym for "Spaniard." (One of the most famous descendants of Galician immigrants is Fidel Castro.)

Galician nationalism, which appeared as early as the 1840s, recalled a mythical Golden Age when the medieval kingdom of Galicia existed. There had indeed been a king of Galicia who was crowned in 1111; the kingdom was partitioned some years later, however, and the southern part was to become Portugal. The northern part fell into disorder until it was incorporated into the kingdom of Castile in 1483.

Despite a study in 1990 stating that 63 percent of the population of Galicia speak and understand *galego* (the Galician spelling of the word for their language), it is not used by the middle and upper classes and is therefore not linked to social progression. Many families now bring up their children to speak Spanish.

Franco was from Galicia, but the region did not profit from the dictatorship. Forgotten or ignored by most governments, as they wield no power, the Galicians are generally mistrustful. Among other Spaniards they have a reputation for caution and guile. However, their region is a joy to visit in the summer. The cooler climate and beautiful views complement the fresh seafood and white wine. You can go from one village festival to the next. The lack of modernization does not generally bother tourists, but, on the contrary, seems to add to the attraction.

Andalusia

Andalusia covers an area of approximately 33,694 square miles (87,268 sq. km), which is 17.3 percent of Spanish territory. This makes it the largest single region, with an area greater than countries such as Belgium or the Netherlands. It is probably one of the best-known regions of Spain, as it embraces the Costa del Sol and its enviable climate. However, the interior is harsh—it is bitingly cold in winter and infernal in summer. Estepa, near Seville, is known as *la sartén* (the frying pan) because of the heat.

Traditionally, much of Andalusia has consisted of vast estates with absentee landlords and casual laborers. Poverty led to migration, especially from the 1950s to the 1970s, and to subsidies by the central government after the dictatorship. (From 1982 and for over ten years the President of Spain was from Seville, and *las malas lenguas*, "spiteful tongues," say that he favored his own region. For instance, expressways in the Basque Country and Catalonia are toll operated, while those in Andalusia are all free.)

The Expo World's Fair at Seville (celebrating five hundred years since the discovery of America) in 1992 was as important to Andalusia as the Olympics were to Catalonia.

The infrastructure was improved and a large part of Seville was modernized. The region now has around 15,000 miles (over 24,000 kilometers) of expressways and highways, and some of the best international airports in the world. The rail links have also improved beyond any expectation, and it is now possible to travel from Seville to Madrid in just two and a half hours.

Despite the modernization of Andalusia, it is still possible to step into a village and sample a taste of the "real" Spain. Nothing can compare with the white villages of Andalusia, sparkling beneath the clear blue skies. Even along the Costa del Sol, the villages of Casares, Manilva, and Mijas are easily accessible.

Andalusia is the heart of the Spanish folklore that is probably best known abroad: here you can find the true magic of flamenco and see bullfighting at its most authentic. Myths like *Don Juan* and *Carmen* were based here. The list of Andalusian festivals is endless, and the openness of the people makes it the ideal place to visit and join in.

Unlike the other regions mentioned above, the people of Andalusia have all the characteristics thought to be most typical of the Spanish. They are friendly, hospitable, generous, and spontaneous, and will always put off whatever they can until tomorrow (*mañana*) so that they can enjoy today. If you are only spending a short time in Spain, this is the place to come. Superficial friendships are their specialty. Everyone is accepted.

MAJOR CITIES

Madrid and Barcelona

Madrid (population 2,984,576) and Barcelona (1,503,451) are the two largest cities in Spain. Madrid has been the capital since the reign of Philip II, in the mid-sixteenth century. Its position in the geographical center of the country is symbolic. Despite the autonomy of all the regions, centralization continues. It may seem a bourgeois, grand, rather suffocating sort of city on first acquaintance. However, it is open to all; its temperament having been formed by the influx of citizens from a diverse country, a large empire, and the accompanying army of bureaucrats.

Barcelona is the largest city on the Mediterranean, and its reputation as the hub of trade is two thousand years old. For many years it was the economic heart of the country, while Madrid was the center of government and administration. Now they compete for the international market.

The 1992 Olympic Games were supremely important for Barcelona, enabling it to prove its professionalism on the international stage. It was also a chance to rehabilitate the old city. A belt of old factories was removed, and the seashore was extended and opened. The roads were improved to make better communications between the city and the rest of the region. The Games were a huge success.

The rivalry between Spain's two preeminent cities is notorious, and nowhere is it more evident than in football. Real Madrid and Barcelona have their fans not only in Spain but also throughout Europe. Since the 1940s their matches overshadow any others played in the country. During Franco's rule a win for Barcelona was seen by the Catalans as a victory against the dictator. Today it is a question of being the best.

Despite the fact that Madrid has the seat of government and the royal family, almost all the ideas that have shaped Spain's modern history—

republicanism, federalism, anarchism, syndicalism, and communism—have found their way into Spain by way of Catalonia. In his book *The New Spaniards,* John Hooper adds that fashions, whether in clothing, philosophy, or art, are usually accepted in Barcelona years before Madrid.

Both cities have a wealth of things for the visitor to do. A visit to Madrid must include the great monuments to history and culture: the Royal Palace, the Prado Museum with its extensive collection of works by Goya, Velasquez, and El Greco, the Reina Sofia Modern Art Museum, home of Picasso's *Guernica,* and the Thyssen-Bornemísza Museum, which traces the history of art from thirteenth-century Italy to modernism. When night falls, Madrid bustles. The bars are full, and overflow on to the pavements on summer evenings. Recharge your batteries at *siesta* time, and prepare to join in the fun.

In Barcelona, take the time to amble through the narrow lanes of the Gothic Quarter, where you will find the imposing cathedral whose construction began in the thirteenth century and continued for the next six hundred years. A stroll down La Rambla takes you past the Liceu opera house, recently renovated after being burnt down in 1994. This promenade is always bustling with shoppers, and street entertainers perform along its length. At its end, the great statue of Christopher Columbus looks out to sea and the new marina stretches before you.

See the Picasso and Miró Museums, and Gaudí's soaring, unfinished cathedral, the Sagrada Família. Then relax at a street café among the amazing buildings, and do a little "people-watching." A busy, cosmopolitan city, where ancient and modern stand side by side, Barcelona will never disappoint you.

chapter two

VALUES & ATTITUDES

The Spanish can sometimes appear to be intensely hedonistic. They seem never to think of tomorrow, but only about enjoying every moment to the full. They are cheerful, friendly, and hospitable.

Perhaps these traits stem from fatalism, for they have little or no faith in institutions, or in established authority, and do not believe they can change things. For centuries the Spanish were militant Catholics, defenders of a faith preaching that suffering in this life brings rewards in the next. Suffering is therefore accepted as a part of life, so when the opportunity arises for pleasure they dive in. An element of risk appeals to them—and they admire the man who faces death in the bullring. The Jesuits, their great teaching order, went where there was the most danger. Heretics were burnt at the stake. Their commitment was all or nothing.

Spain lies on the edge of Europe, and has been cut off from it during different periods. Moorish culture left its mark upon the country—especially in the south, where the Moors remained unconquered for over seven hundred years—and it was said that Africa began south of the Pyrenees. The famous Spanish pride, sense of honor, and *machismo* come from this period. Fighting between various aspirants to the throne kept the Spanish occupied for many years, and the Church's fear of "heresy" held new ideas at bay. Even in the twentieth century, Franco closed the doors to the outside world for much of his dictatorship. Social values were conservative, promoting social order and the traditional Catholic values—bearing hardship in this life in the expectation of a reward in the next; respect for authority; and acceptance of Church teaching on moral questions.

These values were beginning to change even before Franco's death, and they are still changing today. Hundreds of thousands of people had to leave rural areas to find work in the cities, and many others emigrated to France, Germany, and Switzerland. Away from their roots, their ideas began to change. Then tourists started to arrive in increasing numbers, bringing, along with their money, both the materialism and the democratic values of northern Europe. The process of change continues today, as Spain takes its place among the foremost nations of the world.

Spain's Mediterranean climate also exerts a major influence. The summer heat makes it difficult to work, and the balmy evenings are perfect for outdoor socializing rather than staying inside. As in most countries, the further south you go, the more relaxed the people become.

MAÑANA

Mañana does mean "tomorrow" (and also "morning") in Spanish. However, when someone promises to do something for you "*mañana,*" you should be aware that the word is also a synonym for "sometime," which is not necessarily the next day! Things will always happen later than predicted, so never tell a Spaniard your real deadline. Do as everyone else does—exaggerate the urgency, and make a fuss about it. Spaniards find it hard to say no, so they will promise to do something rather than disappoint you. The future is a hazy time for them, with unlimited days in which everything will get done—sometime.

THE FAMILY

In Spain the family is all-important, and family ties are very strong. The elderly are respected, and in some cases three generations still live together. This is changing as families get smaller or have to leave their hometowns, but in general family members still live near each other and maintain contact. An extended family of twenty or thirty people will often gather together to celebrate anniversaries, *santos* (see Chapter 3, Customs and Traditions), and other special occasions.

The Spanish tend to keep their personal lives to themselves, and if there are problems they manage them within the family. For example, mothers, now that they are finally able to work outside the home, often depend on their own parents to help them. Those family members who have moved away can find life difficult when they cannot rely on the family network.

During Franco's dictatorship, Spanish law discriminated strongly against married women. They needed their husbands' approval, known as the *permiso marital*, for almost all economic activities, including employment, ownership of property, or even travel away from home. Significant reforms of this system were begun shortly before Franco's death, and have continued since then. For centuries, the Catholic code of moral values had established stringent standards of sexual conduct for women (but not for men); restricted their opportunities for careers, but honored their role as wives and, most important, mothers; and prohibited divorce, contraception, and abortion, but permitted prostitution. After the return of democracy, the change in the status of women was dramatic. The *permiso marital* was abolished in 1975, the sale of contraceptives was legalized in 1978, and divorce was legalized in 1981. In that same year the parts of the civil code that dealt with family finances were also reformed. Abortion was finally legalized in 1985, but only in certain cases: pregnancy resulting from rape; reasonable probability of a malformed fetus; or to save the mother's life.

By 1984, 33 percent of adult women had entered the workforce and approximately 46 percent of Spain's university enrollment was female. This seemingly painless emancipation of women is due to the fact that for men very little has changed. Women are still expected to run the house and take care of the children with little help from their partners. Since 1970 the size of the average family has decreased from 3.8 persons to 1.36, the lowest in the world after Italy (2.1 is considered necessary for the regeneration of the population), and few children are born outside marriage. Spain now has the lowest marriage rate in the European Union. Many lay the blame for this on a more materialistic society, but it is also a result of women having to balance their workload with their duties at home.

In one thing, however, Spanish women have always been liberated: their name. All Spaniards have two surnames (from both father and mother), so when Pilar Pujol Fernández marries

Jaime Iglesias González, she will not, officially, change her name—although she may be known as la señora de González. On legal documents she will sign her maiden name. Their son, Pepe, will take the first surnames of his father and of his mother, and will be known as Pepe Iglesias Pujol.

Children are an integral part of society. They are not hidden away, but paraded with pride at all hours of the day and night, especially during holiday time. Everyone has time for them, and they receive affection from all sides. There is little emphasis on discipline. Children are loved first and corrected second. This positive nurturing turns them into confident adults who value themselves highly. On the other hand, they take all the attention for granted, and are used to having everything done for them. Young people do not usually leave home before getting married, and although the reason given is the high cost of accommodation, it is probably also the case that they do not want the bother of fending for themselves. They are not usually expected to help with housework, or to contribute financially, even if they are earning good money. Parents are happy to keep them close, and do not want to cut the ties.

Students used to have to study at a nearby university, whereas now they can go to whichever university accepts them. There are more grants available to help them financially, but it remains to be seen whether they will wish to take them up and travel away.

The old values are being questioned: girls have more options when they leave school, fewer people are getting married, and divorce is now available. People are beginning to accept the need for residential homes to care for the sick or the elderly, but still find it difficult to accept help from outside the family. The role of the Spanish family will continue to adapt to the circumstances.

FRIENDS AND ACQUAINTANCES

Spain is one of the friendliest places to visit in Europe. You will be welcomed everywhere, and invited to join in. However, your new Spanish friends probably extend this welcome to all newcomers, and it will rarely lead to anything other than a superficial relationship. Spaniards have many acquaintances, but few friends. Accept that, and enjoy yourself.

Spaniards love talking, and will never miss a chance for conversation. They have very few inhibitions, and do not hide their emotions. They usually rely on their families for emotional support, so outside the home nobody talks about their problems. However, if you do become really friendly with Spaniards you will be considered one of the family. "*Mi casa es tu casa*" ("my house is your house") means just that.

You Mustn't Be Alone!

Sara went to her friend's wedding in a small town near Seville. The wedding was at the beginning of *Semana Santa* (Holy Week), a time of great celebrations in that region. During the meal she was asked where she would be spending the holiday. When she said she would be going back to her apartment alone they were aghast, and she ended up spending the week at the home of one of the guests she had only just met. She was taken to all the local events, and even became an honorary member of one of the local "brotherhoods" (see Chapter 3, Customs and Traditions, Easter).

PRIDE, HONOR, AND *MACHISMO*

Spaniards are proud of their region, and of their lifestyle in general, but they will also point out the negative side of things. Do *not* join in. They are not inviting comments from you, and any negative attitude on your part will be taken personally.

Family pride and honor have always been very important, and an unfaithful wife or pregnant unmarried daughter would lead to shame for the whole family. The word *macho* means male (of any species), and *machismo* describes a certain type of behavior, especially toward women. Under the previous regime the man was the breadwinner and "the king of his castle." He spent much of his time outside the home, with his friends—the bars are still full of large groups of men before and after meals while the women are at home. He did not expect to be questioned about decisions. The woman's place was in the home. She dealt with domestic issues and he neither helped nor interfered in the home. However, as women's role in society is changing, so are men's attitudes.

BEATING THE SYSTEM

In the seventeenth century the "picaresque" novel appeared. It described an anti-hero, or rogue (*el pícaro*) trying to beat the system in a harsh world in any way he could. All Spaniards can identify with him. The difference between rich and poor has been maintained by those who govern, so the Spanish look upon the government and the civil service as the enemy. Nearly forty years under a dictatorship probably did not help. Taxes are levied for the benefit not of the country, but of the government, and are assumed to be lining someone's pocket. There are many proverbs in

Spanish that convey this idea, such as "*Quien hizo la ley, hizo la trampa.*" ("Whoever made the law made the loophole.") There have been countless cases against corrupt politicians who have misused their public position. It is almost expected. So the citizen bends rules and tries his or her luck. Being found out is the only crime here.

The Spanish civil service is an old-fashioned, unwieldy monster. Offices are often open mornings only, and not always daily. Despite long lines the staff (*funcionarios*) will not forgo their leisurely breakfast. You may be sent from one office to another, told to bring four photocopies today, and five tomorrow. However, things have improved since Spain's entry into the European Community.

Studying the Paperwork

Two students arrived in Madrid one weekend, having won a scholarship to study in Spain. They had been told to go to a particular office to arrange to receive their scholarship money. They went there on the Monday morning, to be told after a long wait that they would have to collect various documents from a different office. The other office opened only on Monday and Wednesday mornings. It was closed by the time they got there, so they had to stay two extra days in Madrid—just to get a few papers stamped.

The *Gestor Administrativo*

If you have to deal with officialdom, always take plenty of photocopies, photo ID, and a long book so that you have something to do while waiting in the interminable lines. You will be better treated if you can speak the language, or have a translator.

Best of all, leave it in the hands of a *gestor administrativo*. This is a person who has been trained to advise you on the necessary papers for any transactions with the government. His job is to deal with all this time-consuming paperwork. For instance, to get a driver's license renewed involves going to several offices, waiting in each, and losing a whole morning, at least. Most people will give the necessary documentation to their *gestor*, who will do it for them for a fee.

EGOTISM

The Spanish have very little civic or public spirit, as you can judge from the litter they throw around, or, as another example, the low number of people who give blood. They do not like joining organizations (unless they involve sport). They will do whatever is necessary to further themselves, or their own families, but little or nothing to benefit their local community.

They are suspicious of people, expecting an ulterior motive of personal gain. Ian Gibson, who has lived in Spain since 1978, also adds in his book *Fire in the blood*, "Protest of any kind was futile as well as dangerous in Franco's Spain, and the result is that Spaniards today are still not as energetic as they should be in standing up against petty officialdom." They became fatalistic, and did not bother to question things. The individual does not generally put himself out for the common good. However, the public conscience is being awakened. For example, there have been huge marches throughout Spain against ETA (the Basque terrorist organization), and people came out strongly in 2003 against the war in Iraq.

Work is regarded in a similar vein. It is a necessary evil. The Spanish are not lazy, but they just cannot see what is to be gained by punctuality, by staying late, or by doing more than they are paid to do. In a culture where the individual is important, work comes way down the list of priorities. They can work hard, however, as is evident when they go to other parts of the country or abroad.

TOLERANCE AND PREJUDICE
Spaniards consider themselves tolerant. Friends will voice totally different political opinions, and

this leads to heated arguments but does not affect their friendship. After Franco's death the transition to political pluralism came about with very little violence or vengeance. The Spaniards seem to have buried the past for the good of the present and future, but perhaps this is because the wounds are still raw. (Recently there have been more appeals to investigate particular cases from the Civil War and dictatorship.)

Once state censorship was relaxed on magazines and films in 1976 and in 1978, the market for pornography flourished. In a country where *Playboy* had been outlawed until 1976, this and other foreign "adult" magazines were soon considered tame, and were outsold by Spanish publications. Throughout Spain's large cities, uncensored sex films are readily available in government-licensed "X" cinemas, and prostitutes and brothels freely advertise their services in even the most serious press.

On television, many advertisements are blatantly sexual, and films are not edited even when they are shown during the day. A high level of violence is also tolerated. The television news will carry explicit coverage of death and injury at any time of day. In a country where so many things were banned, it now seems that anything goes.

The Spanish are usually kind and courteous to the foreigners they meet, but perhaps this is

because these foreigners are usually European
tourists, who come to spend money in Spain.
People of a different color are not so easily
accepted. There is also long-standing prejudice
and discrimination against the gypsies, who are
generally considered to be lawbreakers. While
many of them have become part of Spanish
society, others continue to lead their traditional
nomadic way of life. Gypsies were at one time
most numerous in southern Spain, where the
flamenco music and dance that they brought with
them took root. Large communities now exist in
Madrid and Barcelona as well.

RELIGION

Catholicism was the state religion from the Civil
War until the Constitution of 1978. Now Spain
has no official religion, but the Roman Catholic
Church continues to receive financial support
from the state. The vast majority of the
population is Roman Catholic. Yet, by
the 1980s only about 25 percent of
Spaniards regularly attended
church on Sundays. For the
others religion plays little part in life
beyond the formal occasions of going
to Church to be baptized, married
(often to please older relatives), and buried.

However, almost all their customs and traditions
have religious roots.

Those who follow other major religions are
non-Catholic Christians, a rapidly growing
Muslim population (as the number of immigrants
increases), and some Jews.

LIVING FOR THE MOMENT

The Spanish are confident, open individuals with a
zest for life, and for living every moment, that is
contagious. They invite you somewhere because
they really want you to come. They do not want
you to go home because you are all having such a
good time. Who cares about
tomorrow? Now is important.
While there is a good time to
be had, no one will leave.
Night stretches into
morning, and you have some
breakfast before you go home!
You need stamina here, especially if
it is *fiesta* time. People will stay up all night,
drinking and dancing, and then shower and go to
work. If there is time, they will snatch a brief *siesta*
to prepare themselves for the next night. In
Andalusia, you never have a last drink. Instead,
someone will suggest *la penúltima*, the last but one,
because you never refer to the end of the evening.

This exuberance results in a lot of noise. In 1990, 44 percent of Madrid's streets were found to have continuous noise above the rate considered tolerable by the World Health Organization. Mopeds roar around, and horns are honked all the time. In bars there may be several loud conversations going on amid the sound of slot machines and the ever-popular television in the corner.

Spanish people tend to shout. Everyone wants his or her opinion to be heard, and Spanish is a harsh-sounding language. In *The Spanish Temper* Victor Pritchett comments "Castilian (Spanish) is above all a language which suggests masculinity, or at any rate it is more suited to the male voice than to the feminine voice which, in Spain, shocks one by its lack of melody."

If you want to try out your Spanish, don't speak quietly, or you may not even be heard. Pope John Paul visited Spain in 1983 and had to say "*El Papa también quiere hablar*" ("The Pope would like to speak too"), to try and silence the large crowd that had gathered. Spaniards do not seem to be able to stop talking for long. It seems that whatever goes through their mind comes out of their mouths. There is no quiet time here, and Spaniards feel uneasy with silence.

They Can't Keep Quiet!
At the theater one evening, a visitor from
Andalusia could take the suspense no longer, and
shouted an urgent warning to one of the actors
onstage, who was being stalked!

MANNERS

Spanish people can be quite formal until they are
introduced. After that, the rules are relaxed. Once
you are considered a friend, you will be treated in
a warm and familiar way, and polite formulas will
not be necessary. As is the case in many other
countries, you will find that the manners of the
older generation are usually more formal, and a
certain distance should be maintained. Always,
when in doubt, err on the side of good manners.

Women greet each other and men with a kiss
on both cheeks. Men shake hands, and they hug
close friends, loudly slapping each other on the
back at the same time. Spaniards are generally
very tactile people. They will often touch your
arm to emphasize a point or a joke.

At times, however, they may to outsiders seem
discourteous, or even rude. "Please" and "thank
you," considered normal among English-speaking
people, and especially among the British, are
thought to be excessive and unnecessary among

family and close friends, or in everyday exchanges in shops or restaurants . For example, "*Dáme un café*" ("Give me a coffee") is not considered impolite. It is the waiter's job to serve the customer, and no extra niceties are needed.

The Spanish can be very direct once they get to know you. If you are not looking your best today, they will tell you so. They think it, so they say it, and tact does not enter the equation.

However, this directness has its brighter side. The Spanish are the masters of *piropos* (compliments)—to their friends and to the passer-by. In the market, vendors refer to or address women as "*Princesa*" ("Princess") and "*Reina*" ("Queen"), and on the street Spanish men are not shy at showing their appreciation of the female form. A cheerful "*¡Hola, guapa!*" ("Hello, gorgeous!") is often to be heard. Try not to be annoyed; if you ignore the comment, that is as far as it goes. Even better, accept the compliment with a smile, and go on your way.

chapter three

CUSTOMS & TRADITIONS

Spain is steeped in customs and traditions that have been proudly maintained to emphasize differences and preserve regional identity. The year is punctuated by the many *fiestas* that take place, and the participants' vibrant enthusiasm makes every holiday an unforgettable experience. Most of the festivals have a religious origin (Holy Week, the pilgrimages, and the many saints' days), although the social aspect has taken over in most cases. Others are based on historical events or have origins shrouded in the mysteries of time. All these are described in the following pages.

Fiestas can be translated as festivals, public holidays, or just parties. The Spanish are masters of the art of celebrating. Each town has its own festival, usually linked to its patron saint, and often lasting a week. Some of these *fiestas* are internationally famous, such as *Semana Santa* (Holy Week) in Andalusia, or the *San Fermines* (the festival honoring Saint Fermín, famous for the bulls running in the streets) in Pamplona.

PUBLIC HOLIDAYS

Twenty years ago Spain seemed to have one day off after another, but everything is more regulated now and some of the religious festivals are no longer celebrated throughout Spain. Holidays can be divided into four categories: national holidays, applicable everywhere; national holidays that can be replaced in the autonomous communities (political regions); autonomous community (regional) holidays; and holidays of the autonomous communities' capital cities.

NATIONAL HOLIDAYS	
January 1	New Year's Day
January 6	Epiphany
March 19	San José*
May 1	May Day/Labor Day
July 25	Santiago Apostol*
August 15	Feast of the Assumption (not banks)
October 12	Spanish National Day
November 1	All Saints
December 6	Day of the Constitution
December 8	Immaculate Conception
December 25	Christmas Day

The chart shows national holidays. Those marked * can be replaced by the autonomous communities with another date. Each region has its patron saint, and this saint's day is usually chosen.

If a holiday falls on a Tuesday or a Thursday, people will often take an unofficial extra day on the Monday or Friday, giving them a long weekend. This is known as a *puente* (bridge) and is especially common over December 6 and 8. Holidays falling on a weekend are not moved. Most people take their annual vacation in August, and many businesses close for the duration.

THE FESTIVAL CALENDAR

Some of the *fiestas* are just days off, while others can be an excuse for a week of carousing, day and night. Here are a few of the best known:

Christmas (*Navidad*)

Christmas Eve is known as *Nochebuena* (Good Night). A lot of people will go to *La misa del gallo* (midnight mass) even though they do not attend mass at other times. They will have a big family supper that evening and a long lunch the next day. Shellfish and fish will usually be served. Nougat and almond-based cakes are also typical. Most families will have a *belén* (crib) with the holy family, shepherds, and kings. (In Catalonia there is also *el caganer*, a traditional Catalan figurine who is placed squatting in the corner of the Christmas crib, trousers around his ankles—a mixture of the sacred and profane.)

Until recently presents were not received until *los reyes magos* (the three kings) arrived on January 6, but most children have now heard about Santa Claus and also receive presents on December 25, *el día de Navidad*.

El Tió

In Catalonia, children receive presents on December 24 from *el tió*—a log of wood. The children decorate the log, leave the room, say a prayer, and sing a song to *el tió*. Then they go back in, tap him with a stick and find presents under a cloth. *El tió* is actually supposed to *cagar* the presents ("deposit them from his rear end" is the most polite way of saying it). The first time a group of children explained this tradition to me, they all got extra homework as a punishment for being rude in class! I apologized later.

The magical night, however, is still January 5. Towns hold a parade to celebrate the arrival of *los reyes magos*, who ride on horses or camels, attended by their pages, and throw sweets to all the children along the way. That night, before bed, the children leave food and drink out for the kings and their camels, and they will find their presents in the morning.

New Year's Eve (*Nochevieja*) involves another big dinner for family or friends. At midnight the chimes are relayed all over Spain from the Puerta del Sol ("the gate of the sun," the central square in Madrid from which all distances in Spain are measured). Everybody eats twelve grapes, one with each chime. This is to bring you luck in the months ahead. The trick is not to chew, or you will be left with a mouthful of grapes. Just swallow each grape, and go on to the next one! People welcome in the New Year with *cava*, the sparkling wine from Catalonia. After dinner the young people will go out, and may not be back until late the following morning.

San José

St. Joseph's Day, March 19, was once a holiday all over Spain. Now most regions have replaced it with another day. For Valencia, however, it is still important, and in the weeks approaching the festival *las fallas* start to appear in the streets. These are gigantic papier-mâché representations of local, national, and international figures that people have been working on since the previous year. On the day of the *fiesta* the judges decide on the best one, and the others are burned. The festivities begin with the sound of hundreds of firecrackers going off, one after another, shaking the walls and leaving a smell of gunpowder in the air. By the time the fires light the sky the festival is in full swing.

Carnaval

This is the last fling before the penance and sobriety of Lent—the forty days of fasting and penance before Easter. At *Carnaval*, anything goes. During the Civil War Franco abolished it in the conquered rebel areas, as the masked participants could not be recognized. After the war there was still a lot of opposition, so Franco banned it again in 1937. Since 1975, however, *Carnaval* is back, although it is not a big celebration in all areas. Towns have processions at the weekend either before  or after Fat (Shrove) Tuesday. The larger towns have festivities lasting all week. In the Canary Islands, *Carnaval* is celebrated with all the glamour of Rio and its scanty costumes.

Cádiz, in Andalusia, has a very special carnival. As one of Spain's major ports during the sixteenth century, Cádiz copied the carnival of Venice, a city with which it had strong trade links, and since then it has become the liveliest and most dazzling carnival town in mainland Spain, famous for its amusing and creative costumes and satirical song groups. *Carnaval* was never abolished in Cádiz.

Easter

Easter celebrations begin during *Semana Santa* (Holy Week), the week preceding Easter. The best-known celebrations take place in Andalusia, although many towns throughout Spain have religious processions at this time. The processions of Castile (such as at Valladolid and Zamora) are far more austere than those of Seville or Málaga in Andalusia, where different processions take place each day, competing with one another in luxury and splendor.

The parades leave from different churches and wind slowly around the streets, with their lifelike statues of Christ on the Cross, and the Virgin Mary in mourning. *Los pasos* (the huge images representing scenes from Christ's last days) are carried or pushed on wheels by members of the *hermandad* or *cofradía* (religious brotherhoods representing trade guilds or other groups).

The participants spend all year preparing the elaborate costumes and decorations. Penitents wear costumes reminiscent of the Ku Klux Klan, having tall hoods with slits for the eyes. In Andalusia people sing *saetas* (heartrending flamenco songs) to the statues from selected balconies. It can all be very moving, although like everything in Andalusia there is a great deal of other noise and festivity going on too.

There is also a tradition of "passion plays" performed by the locals in several towns since the Middle Ages. They depict the events leading to Christ's Crucifixion.

Sant Jordi

St. George's Day (April 23) is celebrated in Catalonia, where St. George is the patron saint, and is the Catalan version of Valentine's Day. Women receive roses and men books. The roses represent the one that grew from the blood of the dragon St. George killed; the books are given because this is the anniversary of Cervantes' death. This is a recent custom.

Corpus Christi

This feast day, celebrating the Real Presence of Christ in the Eucharist, falls on the first Thursday after Trinity Sunday. In some towns it is a major celebration, usually involving flowers. In the beautiful Andalusian city of Córdoba, the houses are built according to Moorish tradition. There is little adornment on the outside, but the houses look inward on to courtyards full of flowers, and these private patios are open to all on this day. In Sitges, south of Barcelona, certain streets are carpeted with striking patterns made from flower heads, usually carnations.

San Juan

St. John's Eve (June 23), Midsummer's Eve, is a magical night, and there are many associated superstitions. Bonfires are often lit, and the tradition in Málaga is to jump over them for luck as they die down. Perhaps the most famous celebration is the "passing of fire" in San Pedro Manrique, in Soria, where the men of the village walk barefoot over a layer of burning embers without suffering any injury. In Ciutadella, on the island of Menorca, they have *caracoleos,* with riders on rearing horses and games reminiscent of medieval times lending a spectacular air to the festivities.

San Fermín

This is the famous *fiesta* in which the bulls run through the streets of Pamplona, in Navarre, in northern Spain. The week's festival begins officially on July 7, with the ceremony known as *el chupinazo*. The mayor addresses the town, and there are fireworks, a lot of shouting, and many bottles of *cava*. The *encierros* (when the bulls are released from their pens outside the town to run to the bullring) take place daily before each bullfight. The bulls dash through the streets, and the locals run ahead of them, distinguished by their white shirts and red sashes. Many outsiders also run, and there are often injuries. The festivities continue all night long.

PILGRIMAGES AND FAIRS

El Rocío

Andalusia is famous for its *romerías* (pilgrimages) to popular shrines, where *fiestas* are held. Perhaps the most spectacular is the one devoted to *la Virgen del Rocío* (the Virgin of the Dew), popularly called e*l Rocío* for short. Nearly a million people from all over Spain make the long journey to gather in the small hamlet of El Rocío in the marshlands of the Guadalquivir River delta, where the statue has been worshiped since 1280. The pilgrims come on horseback and in gaily decorated covered wagons, transforming the area into a colorful and noisy party. The climax of the festival is the weekend before Pentecost Monday. In the early hours of Monday morning the Virgin is brought out of the church to her pilgrims, who all desperately stretch to touch the statue. This religious fervor is similar to that shown to the *pasos* during *Semana Santa,* and is typical of the Andalusian temperament.

El Camino de Santiago

This has been an internationally famous pilgrimage since the Middle Ages. The apostle James (Santiago) is said to be buried in the town of Santiago de Compostela in Galicia, northwestern Spain, and pilgrims from all over Europe traveled to visit his tomb, coming along *el Camino de Santiago* (the Santiago Way), which runs across the north of Spain. He has been the patron saint of Spain since the time of the Moorish invasion. The pilgrimage began to lose popularity in the fourteenth century, and it was not until 1878, when Pope Leo XIII corroborated

the authenticity of the remains of the Apostle, that there was a gradual resurgence of pilgrimages. The Compostela is an official certificate awarded to all those who make the pilgrimage for religious reasons, but the pilgrim must show proof of having traveled, on foot, by bicycle, or on horseback, a part of the Pilgrim Road—at least a hundred kilometers (sixty-two miles) on foot or horseback or two hundred kilometers (a hundred and twenty-four miles) by bicycle. However, this road is now also a favorite route for walkers with no religious intent.

La Feria de Seville

This takes place two weeks after *Semana Santa* and is the first of the *ferias* (fairs) that are celebrated throughout Andalusia all summer long. The annual *feria* originated in the Middle Ages, when it was the principal means of exchange of local products between towns.

Every town and village in Andalusia has its own *feria*, and it would be possible, if one had superhuman powers of endurance, to spend the whole summer following them about the region. Most other regions have similar *ferias*, generally in August. Different things happen during the day and night. The "day fair" takes place in the streets of the town itself, which is closed to traffic. Businesses close for the week. Tables and chairs are set up, the bars serve food and drink in the street, and music plays on every corner. People of all ages sing and dance, and visitors are welcome.

At night, the fair shifts to the *recinto ferial* (public fairground) on the outskirts of the town. There is a traditional amusement park, with rides for the children, and *casetas* (small marquees) set up by the various clubs, associations, and political parties of the town. Some of these have entertainments, and all have music, room for dancing, and a bar. All night long you will hear the sounds of *sevillanas* (the typical dance) and see the girls dancing gracefully in their traditional long, flounced dresses. Entry to some of the *casetas* is by private invitation only, but there is always a large *Caseta Municipal* put up by the town council and open to everybody. The *ferias* usually start in the middle of the week and finish on a Sunday night. In the larger towns they start at midnight on a Sunday night with fireworks. The Monday after the *feria* is often a local holiday to help everyone to recover from the festivities.

Gigantes y Cabezudos

These are "giants" and "bigheads," who parade through the town during *fiestas*, and have done so at least since medieval times. The giants are usually tall, papier-mâché kings and queens on a frame carried by a bearer, who hides himself beneath the robes. The *cabezudos* wear huge, papier-mâché heads to disguise themselves. The band precedes them through the streets and the *gigantes* follow in quite a stately fashion, while the *cabezudos* dance about or run after the children. They have separate dances that they perform to their own specific music. Many towns have at least one pair of *gigantes*, with several accompanying *cabezudos*.

Dragons, Devils, and Castles

Dracs, diables, i castells (dragons, devils, and castles) sound like elements of a fairy tale, but they are actually the main ingredients of *fiestas* in Catalonia. Fire (*foc*) is an integral part of many traditions, and you should be very careful to keep well back from the parade. The *correfoc* (fire run) takes place in the center of the town, as darkness falls, with the participants dressed up as devils dashing through the streets. They run ahead of a dragon, carrying torches and setting off firecrackers and showers of sparks. They chase the onlookers, so everybody wears hats, scarves, and old clothes. The dragon is made up of people disguised under a long piece of cloth, and breathes fire on all (more firecrackers!). The parade usually ends in a small square where everybody jumps up and down, daring to get as near to the dragon as possible. The wildest of these celebrations is *el patum*, which takes place in Berga, in the mountains north of Barcelona.

Castells (castles), however, have nothing to do with fire. They are part of the day festival and are "human towers." People stand on each other's shoulders to form a castle. The groups compete to form different variations. The top person is always a small child (called the *anxaneta*), who scales the human tower, four or five people high, stands with his or her arm in the air and then slides down almost immediately. They go into training from the time they can walk, and scamper up and down with ease.

Los Moros y Cristianos

The "Moors and Christians" takes place in different towns to commemorate the battle for the town between these two sides. After a few days of mock fighting, the Christians win.

OTHER CUSTOMS

Birthdays (*cumpleaños*) are a bit different in Spain. Children still have parties with presents and cake, but adults are expected to treat people to drinks instead of receiving them. So think hard before you ask a big group to sing "Happy Birthday" to you! Your pockets may be empty by the end of the night.

Santos are similar to birthdays, but they are "name days," when you celebrate the day of the saint after whom you were named. For example, if you are José, it is March 19. Some people may actually have more of a celebration on their name day than they do on than their birthday, especially if their saint is a well-known one.

"Friday the thirteenth" is not unlucky in Spain. Bad luck comes on *martes trece* ("Tuesday the thirteenth").

April 1 in Spain is not All Fool's Day. This falls on December 28, *el día de los inocentes* (the day of the [slaughter of the] innocents), and children play tricks (*inocentadas*) on each other.

These are just some of the many customs and traditions of Spain. Every region has its own, and there is not enough room here to list them all. Sometimes the best festivals are the smaller ones, as the larger ones can be very crowded and full of tourists. If you can go to a local festival with local people, it will be the experience of a lifetime.

FLAMENCO

Spain is known worldwide for its flamenco music and dancing, which are an important part of many *fiestas*. The *gitanos* (gypsies) are the masters of flamenco, and are presumed to have brought it to Spain. Early flamenco seems to have been purely vocal, accompanied only by rhythmical clapping of hands (*toque de palmas*). The guitar was introduced later. Flamenco was first mentioned in literature in 1774. Between 1765 and 1860, the first flamenco schools were founded at Cadiz, Jerez de la Frontera, and Triana, in Seville.

The *cante hondo*, the most serious and powerful flamenco singing, was developed during the golden age of flamenco between 1869 and 1910. From 1915 onward flamenco shows were organized and performed all over the world. There was a lull in popularity, but in 1955 a sort of flamenco renaissance began. Outstanding dancers and soloists soon left the small *tablaos* (flamenco clubs) for the great theaters, and guitar players also began to achieve greater recognition.

BULLFIGHTING

Bullfighting is also a part of many *fiestas*. It began in the Middle Ages as a diversion for the aristocracy when it took place on horseback. By the eighteenth century the poorer population had invented a version on foot. Francisco Romero, who laid down rules for the sport around 1700, is considered the father of bullfighting.

By its fans *la corrida* (the bullfight) is considered an art rather than a sport, technique being very important. It could not exist without the *toro bravo*, a species of bull that is now found only in Spain. There is a strict order to the proceedings. All three matadors' teams are introduced to the public and then the first one takes his place in the ring. There are three parts to the *corrida*:

1. The matador shows his skill by facing the bull and defending himself only with his cape. He is then joined by the picadors, on horseback and armed with lances, who harry the bull.

2. Three helpers (*banderilleros*) each stick a pair of *banderillas* (short spears) into the bull's back.

3. The bullfighter shows his *faena* (mastery), dominating the bull with his red cape. The *corrida* ends as he kills the bull with his sword.

chapter four

MAKING FRIENDS

The Spanish, as we have seen, are renowned for their sociability, friendliness, and hospitality. A large part of their leisure time is spent outside the home. Instead of inviting people to their homes, they meet at favorite bars or restaurants at all hours of the day and night. They love talking, and will strike up a conversation with anyone. The further south you go, the more welcoming they are.

The climate undoubtedly influences their habits. The summer midday sun is braved only by "mad dogs and Englishmen." Most people rest then, because the cool evening is when everything happens. After work they will usually go first to a local bar to wind down, and then home or to a restaurant for dinner. As some people do not finish work until 8:00 p.m., they may not eat until 10:00 p.m., and dinner may last a couple of hours or more. They will then go on somewhere for a few drinks, so even midweek they may not get to bed until 2:00 a.m. You need stamina to keep pace, because you too will be expected to be up early the next day. The Spanish sleep very little.

Those with young children, of course, are more home-based, and may not keep such long hours, but the tendency to stay up late is still strong.

So, how do you get to know the Spanish people? If you are working or studying in Spain, start with your colleagues or classmates. After the formality of a first business meeting, you will soon be on friendly terms. Spaniards usually socialize in big groups of friends or family. Once you become friends with one person you will be asked to come along and join the whole group. You will soon become part of it. However, they will probably not invite you to their homes. Entertaining, as we have seen, usually happens at restaurants. If you are invited to someone's home, take them a good bottle of wine, chocolates, flowers, or little pastries.

If you do not manage to find a group of friends through your ready-made contacts, there are other ways.

LANGUAGE CLASSES

In a country where people love talking, it is almost obligatory to learn their language. More people speak English now, but in general the Spaniards are not very good at foreign languages, and it is a good idea for you to learn some Spanish. A phrase book and a pocket dictionary are good to begin with, but if you plan to stay for a while or will be visiting Spain often, consider doing a basic Spanish course. It will pay dividends. Even if you do not achieve a very high level, any attempt at speaking Spanish will be appreciated.

The Instituto Cervantes (www.cervantes.es) is the Spanish equivalent of the British Council, not only teaching the language but also propagating the Spanish culture. It has branches in many other countries as well as in Spain, and these are the ideal places to attend classes and find out about Spain before you get there.

When you arrive in Spain you can choose from hundreds of different language centers in cities and towns. You will be assessed and placed in the appropriate level. Classes usually include grammar and speaking practice in a small class (four to ten students). Intensive language courses are recommended to get you started. Four hours of classes daily, for a minimum period of two weeks, should give you some confidence and a basic vocabulary to build on.

There are sometimes excursions and other complementary activities. Other students will often have useful tips on how to get to know the locals too. Some schools have Spaniards attending other language classes, and you may see advertisements for people looking for *intercambios* (language exchanges), where you meet informally to help them with English or another language while they help you to perfect your Spanish.

In regions where another language is spoken (the Basque Country, Catalonia, Galicia), a few words in the local language will be appreciated, but no one will expect you to learn that language unless you intend to stay in the area for a long time. Spanish is spoken and understood everywhere, so it makes sense to choose it as your starting point (see Chapter 9, Communicating).

EXPATRIATE CLUBS

It is always a good idea to register with your embassy or consulate, which may be able to give you a list of clubs and associations set up by people from your home country. These can vary, from charitable associations to sports clubs and other groups. Even if you have decided to shun people from back home and embrace Spanish culture, these contacts can be a useful source of recommendations about anything from Spanish classes to doctors, dentists, and workmen.

SPORTS AND OTHER GROUPS

Joining others for sports, hobbies, and other common interests is a good way to get to know other people—and to practice the language. In the local newspapers you will find all types of courses advertised, from cookery to dancing and first aid. Even if you have problems with the language, it is easier to feel confident and comfortable with other people if you are doing something you enjoy and can discuss.

Sports Clubs

Most sports are available in Spain's varied landscape and favorable climate. In the cities there are plenty of gyms, exercise classes, tennis courts, and other sports grounds and facilities. There is usually a joining or membership fee and then an annual or monthly payment. For swimming, there are municipal pools and private clubs in the cities, and swimming competitions to be entered if you are interested. Some gyms also have swimming pools, saunas, and jacuzzis. There are also many golf clubs, especially in the south. Prices vary, and not all are open to the public.

In the winter there is skiing in the mountains. Travel agents can tell you about special deals with ski clubs in the different winter resorts.

THE NEIGHBORS

Try to use the same shops, bars, and restaurants in your locality. People will get to know you, and you will be able to practice speaking with them. The Spanish buy bread every day, and you will soon become one of the locals if you follow their example.

Everyone has a bar where they have breakfast, coffee during the day, and probably a *copita* (little drink) in the evening before going home. Bar staff are used to chatting to the customers, so ask them for information—appeal to their love of their region to find out the best places to see, to visit, and to shop. And be prepared to do your bit by answering their questions about your own country and traditions too.

ENGLISH-LANGUAGE PUBLICATIONS

There are also many English-language newspapers and magazines in Spain. The following is a selection from different areas.

Barcelona Metropolitan (monthly)
The Broadsheet (monthly, all Spain)
Guidepost (weekly, Madrid)
Majorca Daily Bulletin (daily)
Lookout (quarterly, Costa del Sol)
Island Connections (fortnightly, Canary Islands)
Sur in English (weekly, Málaga)

chapter five

THE SPANISH AT HOME

Today most Spaniards live in towns or cities, chiefly in Madrid and in the coastal towns. Only 53 percent of the population lived in towns in 1953, but by 1980 this had risen to 75 percent. The figure has varied very little since then.

SPANISH HOMES

The majority of Spaniards, who live in cities and large towns, live in apartments (*pisos*). An apartment may be a huge property on one of the nation's most exclusive streets, or a modest, three-bedroomed affair in a high-rise block. The older buildings traditionally had a caretaker (*conserje*), who lived on the ground floor and kept an eye on things, but there are very few of these left now.

In many of the smaller towns and villages people live in houses, and town houses are now in vogue even in suburban areas. These are small, three-story houses with the living area on the upper two floors and a garage on the ground floor. There is not always a garden.

In rural areas people live in houses that vary greatly from one area to another. Local stone is used, and each area has its particular style. In Andalusia, white houses are built around beautiful patios, reflecting the influence of Moorish architecture.

More Spaniards own a second home than in any other country in the European Union. Perhaps this is partly because many who left their villages and towns to work in the larger towns and cities did not sell their family homes. Every weekend city-dwellers leave the cities in droves to go to their villages or little apartments outside the city. Outside Madrid you will see complexes (*urbanizaciones*) of these apartments with swimming pools, tennis courts, and everything to make them the perfect vacation home. Many Madrid families spend their summer vacations here while the father remains in the city, joining them on weekends.

Spain has very few rented properties, compared to other European countries. This is due to government policies rather than choice. Franco froze rents in 1936 and allowed tenants to pass on their leases to any relatives living with them at the time of their death. It was not until the 1980s that the government altered the legislation to allow landlords to raise rents in accordance with the cost of living, and some tenants are still paying a pittance, even in very expensive areas. Because landlords still cannot sign a new, up-to-date lease with the occupants, they are very wary of new tenants and will often insist on one-year contracts. It is difficult to evict a troublesome tenant, so although almost a quarter of the population owns a second property very few of these are available to rent. The cost of housing, and the lack of rental property, is one reason why Spaniards live at home until they buy their own apartment—usually when they marry.

Although the government has helped with subsidized housing and low-interest loans, most of this housing is, and always has been, for sale, not for rent. Prices have never been cheap, and thus the poorest people, who continue to rent, have been kept out of the housing market altogether.

THE HOUSEHOLD

In general, the domestic duties are the wife's domain. Although the father is nominally the head of the household, the mother is the real boss in the home. Even working women are dedicated housewives. They are extremely house-proud, and although many apartment complexes may look neglected from the outside, they will be sparkling inside. Daughters may help a little, but sons are usually excused. Some men do help in the house, of course, but women still do the lion's share. In Catalonia, *fer dissabte* ("to do Saturday") refers to the extra cleaning done on a Saturday when there is more time.

In all parts of Spain people eat a Mediterranean diet. Said to be one of the healthiest diets in the world, it includes plenty of fruit, vegetables, fish, meat, and, of course, olive oil. It will differ from one region to another, depending on what is available locally. People use fresh produce whenever possible, and regard preprepared food as inferior. In a Spanish apartment complex, the smell of cooking pervades the air from early morning, as intricate dishes are prepared.

The mother traditionally used to hover around the table, clearing one course away to produce the next, and eating when she could. However, as more women join the workforce and fewer grandmothers are living nearby to help, this is changing. People do cook things from scratch, if necessary starting the cooking the previous evening and finishing it on the following day, but this involves a great deal of work, and most working women are now cutting down, where they can, on the hours spent in the kitchen.

THE DAILY SHOPPING

Most small shops open from 9:00 a.m. to 1:00 or
2:00 p.m., and close for the *siesta*. They reopen
from 5:00 p.m. to 8:00 p.m. Larger stores,
especially in the cities, usually stay open all day.
Shops in some towns have Monday closing or
may open only half the day on Saturdays. Tourist
areas may have a very different timetable, staying
open late at night when people are home from the
beach and out for an evening stroll.

The women still do their shopping daily in
local shops. Even those who are working will buy
the bread or meat on the way home. They may go
to supermarkets to stock up on some basic goods,
but they will still have a favorite butcher and
baker and a preferred fruit and vegetable stand at
the local market. They drive a hard bargain and
make the shop assistants earn their money.

Spanish fishmongers
will do everything
except cook the fish,
and butchers will
cut, skin, slice, and
prepare to order.

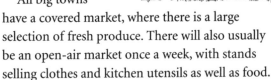

All big towns
have a covered market, where there is a large
selection of fresh produce. There will also usually
be an open-air market once a week, with stands
selling clothes and kitchen utensils as well as food.

The stands are usually no cheaper than the local stores, and are probably not the place to find great bargains. Sometimes the gypsies will bargain, but never for food. Prices are set.

The Spanish do not believe in standing in line, although the storekeepers seem always to know whose turn it is. In some supermarkets there is a system of tickets for the meat counter—you take a ticket and wait for your number to be called before being served.

Every town has an emergency twenty-four-hour pharmacy (*farmacia*) service available. You will need a prescription from the doctor and may need to be escorted by the local police if it is late at night (to prevent drugs being stolen). All pharmacists display the address of the pharmacist on duty.

Banks are usually open on weekday mornings until 2:00 p.m. Money can also be exchanged in *oficinas de cambio* (exchange offices) in most seaside areas. Rates may vary greatly between one place and the next.

DAILY LIFE

Despite staying up late, most Spaniards start their days early, at 7:00 or 8:00 a.m. Breakfast at home can be quite perfunctory, as most people prefer to have a sandwich or pastry later in the morning.

This usually involves a trip to the local bar, where the waiters will be kept frenetically busy for an hour or so.

At 1:00 p.m. most people leave work, and many will drop in for a *tapa* (snack) back at the bar before heading home for their lunch around 2:00 p.m. Traditionally, lunch is followed by a nap— the famous *siesta*—but, because most people now commute further between home and work, this custom is in decline. However, if they can get home for lunch the long break will allow for that *siesta*. The main daily television news is broadcast at this time, as are some of the most popular programs, including the melodramatic *culebrones* (soap operas) from South America. Factory workers may be back to work in two hours, but store assistants and many others will not return until 5:00 p.m.

Most businesses close at 8:00 p.m. Once again, the bars are buzzing with people having a *cervezita* (little beer) before going home. The evening meal will be after 9:00 p.m. It will be lighter than the midday meal, and will be eaten out or at home with the family. People will often stay up until well past midnight, and in the summer you may see them sitting outside their houses *tomando el fresco* (enjoying the cool air) and passing on the local news. Although the Spanish are extremely friendly, they do not readily invite people to their homes—socializing is done outside the home. Even teenagers are more likely to meet at the local *plaza* (square) than in one of their bedrooms.

EDUCATION

Education is very important for the Spanish. It is worth noting that the translation of the word "polite" is *bien educado,* well educated. Education is a means of bettering oneself. There has always been a feeling that one's children should do something better than manual labor, and the majority of Spanish parents want their children to go on to a college or university.

Just under half the children in Spain attend private schools. These are now almost all state-funded, and range from exclusive, bilingual educational establishments to schools where the teachers may have no other recommendation than being related to the principal. Public schools are controlled more strictly by the state. Until recently there were two types of school: BUP (*Bachillerato Unificado Polivalente*), leading to university, and FP (*Formacion Profesional*), leading to manual jobs. However, education is now compulsory until the age of sixteen, and all children go to one type of school. New subjects have been introduced in an attempt to bring about changes in traditional thinking (environmental conservation, peace studies, sexual equality), languages are taught earlier, from seven or eight years of age, and the emphasis is on confidence building, although the final exams have stayed more or less the same.

Children usually attend school from three years of age, although it is not obligatory until the age of six. They have a very long day. Primary school begins at 9:00 a.m. and ends at 1:00 p.m. There are more classes from 3:00 to 5:00 p.m., and many children then go on to extracurricular activities. Most families have lunch together, but younger children may be in bed before dinner is served, so they have an early light meal (*la merienda*). Their day may be only slightly shorter than the normal school day. Secondary school begins at 8:00 a.m., and on one day there are no afternoon classes. Most teenagers eat with their parents and also go to bed late, having fitted homework and other activities into the evening.

There are now more grants being paid to students, although a study at the University of Barcelona showed that half of the students there still have to work as well as study. In the past many students worked in the mornings and studied in the evenings, or *vice versa*. There was no time limit for finishing a course, so people would stay at college for as long as necessary.

Students once had to go to their local university, but may now choose where to study. There is still a shortage of places, as there are many young people, better educated than before, competing for them. However, this will change in the future as, since the 1970s, the Spanish birthrate has decreased from one of the highest in Europe to the lowest.

TELEVISION

In summer the Spaniards spend a lot of time out of doors, but in winter they watch a great deal of television—more than three hours a day. Even when no one is watching it, the television is often left on. At lunchtime and in the mornings the South American soaps (*culebrones*) top the ratings; there are more and better home-produced programs on in the evenings. There is now a range of Spanish sitcoms and series that rival imported shows. Approximately 70 percent of the Spanish form their political views from what they hear on television, so *la caja tonta* (the silly box) is more than just a form of entertainment.

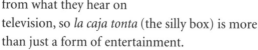

There are two national channels—TVE1 and TVE2. Some autonomous regions also have their own channels, but these vary in quality. Catalonia's two channels are in Catalan, while the Basque Country has one in Basque and one in Spanish. Private channels have existed since late 1989, and there are now three: Antena 3, Tele 5, and Canal Plus (pay channel). The competition has lessened the public television's advertising revenue, and as a result government funding has had to be increased. *Televisión Española* encompasses not only television but also several radio stations, and the national orchestra and choir. Satellite television is also widely available.

THE PRESS

The Spanish do not buy as many newspapers as people do in other European countries, but this seems to be a phenomenon of Mediterranean societies, where the oral tradition still reigns. Most bars provide a handful of newspapers for their clients, and it would be difficult to calculate how many people read any one newspaper. In general, Spain has quality newspapers and nothing to equate to the tabloids and gutter press of other countries. The daily sports papers *As* and *Marca* are very popular.

There are, however, a large number of magazines covering all interests. One example is *¡Hola!*, avidly read in Spain since 1944, which is based on photo shoots and interviews with the famous. In 1988 an English version, *Hello!*, was launched, and has also become enormously popular. During the transition from the Franco dictatorship the end of censorship led to a totally different type of magazine, *Interviú*, which "set out to provide its readers with the two things they had been denied under Franco—uninhibited coverage of politics and pictures of naked women," John Hooper comments in his book *The New Spaniards*. It contains word-for-word interviews with politicians, interspersed with sexy photos. For the non-Spanish reader some of its full-color features, which have explicit, brutal photos of killings and accidents, can be shocking.

The kiosks in the main streets will show the huge range of reading material available. The Spaniards may not buy many newspapers, but that does not mean they do not read.

TIME OUT

Spanish sociability is legendary. Free time is spent with friends and family, and most people are out more often than they are at home. As they say, *viven en la calle* ("they live in the street"). Most working women devote Saturday mornings to housework, but at other times they go out, for shopping, family visits, or other socializing. Many people who live in the cities have second homes on the coast or in the mountains, where they spend weekends and holidays. The resulting traffic jams back into major cities on Sunday evenings are best avoided.

SHOPPING FOR PLEASURE

As in many other countries, in Spain shopping is a pleasant pastime as well as a necessity. In the cities you will find fashion boutiques and department stores, such as El Corte Inglés, and even Marks & Spencer. These will be open all day, often until 9:00 p.m. Shops open only three or four Sundays a year, mainly around Christmas time. However, you can always do as many Spanish people do, and *mirar los escaparates* (go window-shopping).

Markets are very popular in Spain, and there are open-air and covered markets in most towns. On weekends you will find flea markets, with an abundance of knickknacks and crafts. The most famous of these is the huge Sunday morning *rastro* that takes place in the center of Madrid, and is well worth a visit. There are many stands to browse through, and as you walk around the streets you will find plenty of bars open for breakfast, brunch, or lunch.

EATING OUT

It is a widespread custom to go for a *tapa* before meals. These snacks are often smaller-sized versions of proper meals, and are the ideal way to taste unusual dishes. There are hundreds of different *tapas,* but a few typical ones are *champiñones al ajillo* (mushrooms in garlic sauce), *tortilla de patatas* (Spanish omelette), *pescadito frito* (small fried fish), and *pulpo a la gallega* (octopus in paprika sauce). Spaniards will often go to several different bars, tasting the *tapas* and drinking a glass of wine or a small glass of beer in each one. In Andalusia, particularly, people usually stand at the bar, and do not stay long in any one place.

You may notice that some of the best bars look rather scruffy, with a lot of papers and nutshells all over the floor. This is because people just throw their paper napkins on to the floor after they have finished—it is not that the sweeping has been neglected. A bar that has a messy floor means that it has a large clientele, and is therefore likely to be good.

In tourist areas the bars will often have menus with photographs of the dishes to avoid language problems. These will usually be *platos combinados*, with everything served on one plate. Eating outside on the *terraza* is lovely, but it is worth noting that you will probably have to pay a little more for this prime position.

The Spanish love eating. They eat late in the day, and take their time over a meal. In tourist areas the restaurants will cater to the foreigners and open earlier, but elsewhere they do not expect anyone to want lunch before 2:00 p.m., and dinner will not happen until 9:00 or 10:00 p.m. All restaurants usually open for both lunch and dinner, and serve three-course meals at both, although people usually eat less at one meal than the other, except perhaps on weekends or when they are on vacation.

There are all kinds of eating-places, from small, family-run bars to large, expensive restaurants, and you can eat well in any of them—the best food is not necessarily to be found at the most expensive restaurants. The Spaniards love their food, and are knowledgeable about their local dishes, often traveling to small restaurants off the beaten path for regional specialties.

In the popular restaurants, overworked waiters run between tables, but you will not have to wait too long. At lunchtime there is the *menú del día* (set menu of the day), which has a selection of dishes at a modest price. If you want to choose from the more expensive *à la carte* menu, ask for the *carta*. The variety of food available is often amazing.

TIPPING

The Spanish hardly ever tip. Some expensive restaurants may add a service charge of 10 to 15 percent. Smaller restaurants and bars do not. If you feel the service has been particularly good, you can round up the bill to the next euro or leave a few coins out of the change. In the bigger cities, however, tourists may be expected to be more generous than locals.

With people who provide a service, such as taxi drivers, hairdressers, and barbers, it is usual to round up the bill with a few coins.

On Sundays the *Merenderos* (reasonable roadside restaurants) are usually full of big family parties. *Chiringuitos* (the seaside version) are as near to the beach as possible. Bars selling food will be open from early morning until late at night. Much of the food is quite elaborate, and needs a lot of gentle cooking.

You will not normally find either bread plates or butter on the table, though bread on its own is always served. Water is not usually brought unless you ask for it, and then it will be bottled. Drink it from the water glass—larger than the wine glass.

FOOD AND DRINK

Spanish cooking varies greatly from region to region. Catalan and Basque cuisine is considered to be the most elaborate and prestigious. Spanish food is frequently thought to be very spicy, but this is not the case; in general the most piquant ingredient is paprika. The most widely eaten meat is pork (*cerdo*), but in much of the country lamb (*cordero*) is eaten on special occasions. Spaniards have long consumed large amounts of fish (*pescado*) and seafood (*mariscos*). Legumes, especially lentils (*lentejas*) and chickpeas (*garbanzos*), also form an important part of the diet.

Every region has its specialty. Around the *costas* (coasts) it is usually fish. In Málaga it is the small fish—*pescaditos, sardinas, boquerones*—while in the North (especially Galicia and the Basque Country) the seafood is wonderful—*pulpo a la gallega* (octopus), *xangurro* (Basque crab), *bacalao al pil-pil* (cod fried in garlic and served in the sauce) are only a few examples. Valencia has *paella*, one of Spain's most famous dishes: saffron-flavored rice with vegetables and seafood, or chicken.

Inland, they serve meat. A traditional meat stew is found in Madrid (*cocido madrileño*), Catalonia (*escudella*) and Andalusia (*potaje*). Meat, legumes, and vegetables are stewed and served in three courses: first the broth, then the vegetables, and finally the meat. In central Spain *cordero* (lamb), *cochinillo* (suckling pig), and *jamones* (cured hams) are the specialties. In Catalonia there is a wonderful variety of cold meats and sausages (*butifarra*), less spicy than the *chorizo* (paprika sausage) from the south. There are many, many more dishes, including, of course, *gazpacho*, the delicious cold tomato and garlic soup of Andalusia.

Garlic and olive oil are widely used in Spanish cuisine, and everywhere you will see cured hams hanging from the roof or waiting to be sliced behind the bar. This *jamón serrano* is a delicacy prized above ordinary ham (*jamón de York*).

TABLE MANNERS

Table manners are not very different from those in other Western countries, but the following are worth noting:

- Keep both hands in view above the table. It is not considered polite to rest one hand on your lap while eating with the other.

- It is not polite to put something into your mouth and then take it out again, so people break off pieces of their bread, rather than bite into it.

- Prawns can be picked up with the fingers to be eaten.

- The Spanish hold the fork in the left hand and the knife in the right, and do not switch them. Food is pushed on to the fork with the knife.

- When you have finished, place your knife and fork side by side on the plate.

- People usually wipe their mouths with their napkin before drinking.

- A typical toast will consist of the host raising his or her wineglass and saying, "¡Salud!"

Alcohol

The most famous wine of Spain is, of course, sherry, from Jerez de la Frontera, in Andalusia. Sherry is fortified with grape spirit and classified according to type—the pale, delicate *fino*, through *manzanilla*, *amontillado*, and *oloroso*, to the dark, rich, and fragrant *palo cortado*. You will find the Andalusians themselves enjoying their crisp, chilled *fino* or *manzanilla* at *fiesta* time.

The best red wines (*vino tinto*) come from Rioja, Ribero del Duero, and Navarre (Navarra) in the north. The top white wines (*vino blanco*) are from Rueda and Penedés in Catalonia. As you get to know Spanish wines you will also discover a whole range of lesser-known wines as well as the brandies and sherry from Jerez , the *pacharán* of the Basque Country, and the sparkling *cava* from Catalonia. There is also *sidra* (cider) in Asturias, and *sangría* (a kind of wine punch) throughout the country. Spain also produces beer, but this is not drunk with meals. It can be ordered at the bar with *tapas*.

To end a meal, most people will order a cup of coffee. Perhaps it will be a *café solo* (espresso)—but you may like to try a *carajillo*, which is coffee laced with brandy or the spirit of your choice. Just ask for a *carajillo de* . . . (Baileys, for instance). ¡*Salud!*

Despite the amount of alcohol you see around you in Spain, you will not see many drunks. The

Spanish do not like to lose their dignity: they drink, but not so much that they are out of control. Perhaps it is precisely because there is so much alcohol around. Most homes have wine on the table, and children may drink it (heavily watered down) from an early age. In some areas the *porró* (a glass carafe with a long spout that you hold up and aim at your mouth) will be in the center of the table for you to help yourself—not an easy thing to do! Things may be changing, but it is still the minority that drinks to get drunk.

NIGHTLIFE

Bars in Spain are open all day and most of the night. Most will have closed by 2:00 or 3:00 a.m., but then there are always the *discotecas* to move on to. Many of these are free for women. Otherwise, the entrance fee will usually include one free drink, but further drinks will be much more expensive than in a bar. The *discotecas* usually close at 5:00 a.m., when people go on for hot chocolate and *churros* (rather like doughnuts) before going home.

You can also visit a *tablao*—a flamenco club. Andalusia is the home of flamenco, but as the Andalusians moved around, so did their music, and there are now *tablaos* all over Spain. The *gitanos* (gypsies) are still the greatest exponents of flamenco. Tourists throng the well-advertised shows, which have troupes of smoldering dancers with long, flounced dresses and castanets. However, the locals will probably go to a much smaller place where the *artistes* may be older, less easy on the eye, and less acrobatic, but they will have *arte*, and that is all that matters.

What Is Arte?

In a small *tablao* in Málaga, there is a stout woman in her late fifties who walks slowly and heavily on to the stage. She does not look like a dancer. But then the music starts, and she comes alive. She draws herself up, assumes a disdainful expression, lifts her skirts, stamps her feet, and whirls herself into the music. She is a mistress of the art, and she mesmerizes the audience. That is *arte*.

CULTURAL ACTIVITIES

The local tourist offices have a wealth of information on local museums, galleries, and other places of interest, and on current events. Also, in Madrid and Barcelona, the magazine *La Guiá del Ocio* will tell you everything that is currently going on in those cities. Smaller towns announce their local events in the newspapers.

The Spanish may not all go frequently to museums or art galleries, but they do appreciate and value *cultura*. Most people have a basic knowledge of artists and art history, especially that which is relevant to their local area.

Museums and Galleries

These are also listed in the entertainment guides. It is worth noting that most are closed on Mondays. The state museums are free to Spanish nationals, but some have free admission (*entrada gratis*) on Sundays for everyone. Madrid boasts the enormous Prado museum, which houses paintings by El Greco, Goya, and Velasquez, among many others. Picasso's famous *Guernica* can be seen in the nearby Reina Sofia museum of modern art. In Barcelona there are the Picasso and Miró museums, and Bilbao is the site of the

 new Guggenheim museum, worth a visit to see the building alone. The major national museums are in the large cities, but many

smaller Spanish towns often have interesting museums that cover their local history, arts, crafts, and traditions.

Historic Buildings and Antiquities

Spain is full of historic places to visit.
Monumental remains of the Roman occupation
can be seen throughout the country: the city walls
of Lugo, the aqueducts at Segovia and Tarragona,
the theater and public buildings at Mérida, the
bridges at Alcántara and Córdoba, and the towns
of Italica and Ampurias (Emporion) are all prime
examples. There is also an example of an Iberian
settlement at Ullastret, in
Catalonia. Andalusia has
Moorish remains such as
the *mezquita* (mosque) of
Córdoba, the Alhambra
palace of Granada, and the
Alcázar (fortress) of Seville.
Every city has its old part,

and there are some towns, such as Toledo,
Salamanca, and Cuenca, where nearly every
building seems worthy of mention.

Barcelona's open-air *Poble Espanyol* is laid out
as a small town—you walk through the streets
and see replicas of famous buildings from
different parts of Spain. You can appreciate the
various architectural styles of Catalonia, then turn
a corner to see a model of the Giralda in Seville.

In cathedrals and other places of worship,
people are expected to dress modestly (covering
legs and arms) and behave respectfully.

Theater, Opera, Dance, and Music

The Spanish love to go to the theater. All cities have several theaters, and many towns also have small ones, where local companies perform. Opera and dance can be seen in the cities, and Spain is now on the concert trail of most international stars. The Spanish attitude toward most cultural events is quite relaxed, and people do not dress very formally, except for the opera.

Theaters put on a variety of plays ranging from the classical Golden Age plays of Calderón de la Barca and Lope de Vega to any of Lorca's twentieth-century dramas, such as *Bodas de sangre*, *Yerma*, or *La Casa de Bernarda Alba*, or translations of international hits such as *Germans de Sang*, the Catalan version of *Blood Brothers* by Willy Russell, or *Arte* (*Art*) by Yasmina Reza.

Spain has made a lasting contribution to the world of opera and song with the well-loved Spanish tenors Plácido Domingo and José Carreras, and the soprano Montserrat Caballé, who are all internationally famous. You will find the classical operas occasionally performed, and there is also *Zarzuela*, "light" opera similar to the operettas of Johann Strauss or the works of Gilbert and Sullivan.

Dance encompasses both "ballet español" (a mix of ballet and flamenco) and classical ballet, with Victor Ullate and Nacho Duato. Flamenco itself also has its internationally famous, such as the dancer Joaquín Cortes and the guitarist Paco de Lucia.

The most famous Spanish composers are Enrique Granados and Isaac Albéniz, Manuel de Falla and Joaquín Rodrigo. Andrés Segovia is considered the father of classical guitar.

The major cities all have festivals of theater and music, either over the summer months or integrated into the celebrations of their patron saint. Madrid has its festival in May, with both local and international stars. In Barcelona the "Grec" in July and August brings many international stars to the city.

Pop Music

Today, Enrique Iglesias (whose father Julio enthralled a previous generation of girls) is one of the best-known pop stars internationally. In Spain there are many groups, but few are known outside the country.

In 2003 millions of Spaniards stayed at home to watch the grand final of the blockbuster talent show *Operación Triunfo* (Operation Victory). It was noted at one point that more than fifteen million people were glued to their screens—a record in Spanish broadcasting history.

Cinema

The cinema, of course, is hugely popular. Most of the films shown are American, and they are dubbed into Spanish. Original version cinemas, where the films are not dubbed, are getting more popular, but you will find them only in the cities. They will be marked "v.o." (*versión original*) in the newspapers. The home-produced films are well worth watching if your Spanish is good enough to follow them. In the summer some small towns

 will have *el cine de verano*, films shown in the local *plaza* (square). When it starts getting dark you will see people heading to the square with chairs under their arms, although some seating may be supplied. The films will be in Spanish, but the atmosphere is great.

Spanish cinema in general is relatively unknown internationally, although the films of the director Luis Buñuel, full of dark surrealism, anarchy, and wit, enthralled the world's cinemagoers from the late 1920s onwards. Today the actors Antonio Banderas and Penélope Cruz are famous, as is Spain's best-known director, Pedro Almodóvar, who was the most internationally successful member of *la movida madrileña* (the Madrid "scene") of the 1980s. This term describes the new artistic activity and atmosphere during the transition from Franco's dictatorship to democracy. The "scene" centered on the nightclubs, where people congregated until the early hours and brought together many new young music groups and people involved in other arts. It has sometimes been compared to London's "swinging sixties."

SPORT

The Spanish love sport, and, as in most European countries, soccer reigns. They love both playing it and watching it. Every town has its playing field, although only in the north do they have the luxury of grass (except for the professional stadiums). They also play basketball, tennis, golf, and a whole range of other sports, including *balonmano,* which has goalposts as in football, but the ball is thrown, not kicked. In the Basque Country there are sports that exist nowhere else. These are similar to Scottish games, such as "tossing the caber"—throwing a large, heavy, wooden pole as far as you can—and involve great physical strength.

Soccer was introduced into Spain by the British in the second half of the nineteenth century and a professional league was set up in the 1920s. By the 1950s soccer had surpassed bullfighting (which had been the most popular spectator sport from the eighteenth century) in popularity. Spain's leading clubs have a distinguished record in international competitions, although the national team has not done as well. Besides supporting a local team, everyone in Spain supports either Real Madrid or FC Barcelona.

At the end of the 1980s, soccer was challenged by basketball, whose popularity soared after Spain won the silver medal in the sport at the 1984 Olympics. There is a popular league, ACB (Basketball Clubs Association). The main teams are Real Madrid (who have won several European Leagues or Cups), Barcelona CF, Joventut, and Estudiantes. They all have international players.

Over twenty years ago the success of tennis players Orantes and Santana made this game more popular. Nowadays, Arantxa Sanchez, Conchita Martinez, Alex Corretja, and Sergi Bruguera are international players and there are public tennis courts all over the country.

There are also a lot of cycling clubs, especially in the north. Miguel Indurain won five "Tours de France," and several other first-class professionals have now taken his place, including Abraham

Olano. Although Spain is a very mountainous country and most cities are not provided with bicycle lanes, nearly every teenager has a bicycle.

Other popular spectator sports include motorcycle racing, swimming, Formula 1 car racing, and hockey on roller skates.

Walking

The Spaniards are active users of their parks and countryside. Apart from the famous *Camino de Santiago* (see Chapter 3, Customs and Traditions), there are many walking routes all over Spain. *Excursionista* clubs or groups of friends take to the mountains and nature reserves every weekend to enjoy the wonderful scenery. There is usually a meal at the end of it! On many mountain peaks you will see *hermitas*, small chapels dedicated to saints venerated in that area. It is worth braving the winding roads for the amazing views. At least once a year there will be a pilgrimage there that turns into a kind of town picnic, with communal *paella* or shared lunches. Some *hermitas* have a bar or restaurant attached.

Unfortunately, as a nation, Spain does not have a good record for protecting its natural resources. Every summer there are numerous forest fires, many of which are started deliberately. Overall, Spain has the worst record in the EC for violating environmental protection.

LOTTERY AND GAMBLING

The Spanish are a nation of gamblers. Perhaps this is because they love excitement and taking risks, inherent in Spain in everything from bullfighting to driving, or perhaps it is simply the hope of making easy money. Whatever it is, there are more types of lottery, and bigger prizes to be won, in Spain than in any other country.

The oldest lottery, *la lotería nacional,* has been running since 1812. It earns half its money from the two Christmas lotteries: *el gordo (*the fat one), just before Christmas, and *el niño* (the child) on January 5, the day before *los reyes magos* bring the presents. These carry the biggest prizes, and in 1991 it was estimated that their takings ($1,542 million, or £867 million) represented an average outlay of $50 (£28) per Spanish adult. Everyone takes part, and the winning numbers are sung out on national television in a kind of Gregorian chant for several hours. Wherever you go on December 23 you will hear it.

There are other national lotteries, and also regional ones. The ONCE kiosks can be seen all over Spain. They are owned by the *Organización Nacional de Ciegos Españoles* (National Organization for the Blind). This was created by Franco's government in 1938 to provide employment for the blind, and was exempt from tax. The blind sellers would stand on street corners with their tickets. By 1950 ONCE was able to provide a welfare system for its members, and new management meant it became more streamlined and successful. Today it is a great financial empire.

Apart from the lotteries, a vast amount of money is spent on slot machines (*tragaperras*), which can be heard bleeping away in the corner of every Spanish bar—and  bursting into a lively tune when you ignore them. In 1991 their net takings dwarfed that of the lottery (over $2 billion, or £1.5 billion). Even bingo is enthusiastically played in Spain, but it is very strictly controlled, and played only in casinos, where you have to produce ID before being admitted.

chapter seven

TRAVELING

FLYING

Spain has a number of international airports.
Apart from the major airports of Madrid
(Barajas) and Barcelona (El Prat), there are
smaller ones, many of which serve the tourist
resorts along the Mediterranean coast. The
national airline, Iberia, and the smaller airline
Aviaco operate a network of internal flights. The
puente aereo (air bridge) that links Madrid and
Barcelona is the most important internal air
route. Barajas, in Madrid, handles over twenty-five
million passengers a year, a figure set to almost
double by 2010. To cope with this increase in traffic
a new satellite terminal is planned in addition to
two new runways, making four in all. In the
meantime, however, there are frequent delays.

DRIVING

Spaniards drive quickly and aggressively, and have
no patience. You need to be constantly alert, and to
use your mirrors all the time. You are expected to

know where you are going, and people will sound their horns if you hesitate for even a moment.

Buy a good map, and try to work out your route before leaving home. In some areas towns will have their names in the local language. This can be confusing in the Basque Country, for example, where San Sebastian becomes Donostia and Vitoria is Gasteiz.

Legal Requirements

To drive a car in Spain you must carry with you your passport, or some other form of ID, your current driver's license, valid insurance papers, and the vehicle registration document. You should also have two red warning triangles, a first aid kit, a fire extinguisher, and a set of spare bulbs.

The use of seat belts is compulsory.

The police are more vigilant than they used to be about violations of traffic laws, and on-the-spot fines are compulsory for nonresidents. Other fines are calculated according to the severity of the offense and the opinion of the police officer.

The legal drunk driving limit is 0.05 percent (0.5 grams per liter), and Breathalyzer tests are frequent all over Spain. Make sure you are aware of speed restrictions—there are many speed traps.

It is illegal to use a mobile telephone while driving, although you can pull over to the side of the road for an emergency call. Motorists are required to use a hands-free kit, without earphone connections, fitted to the power supply of the car. Those who break the law face fines of up to 300 euros (around $300).

The Roads

There are all types of roads, from fast modern highways to narrow, country roads. They are:

Autopistas, A or E (expressways). These are often toll roads. Speed limit 75 mph (120 kmph).

Autovias (divided highways, or dual carriageways). These sometimes have only a central barrier, sometimes a wider safety zone. Speed limit 62 mph (100 kmph).

Carreteras Nacionales, N or CN (main roads). Speed limit 62 mph (100 kmph) where there is a hard shoulder and 56 mph (90 kmph) where there is none.

Carreteras Comarcales, C (country roads). Speed limit 56 mph (90 kmph).

Carreteras Locales (by-roads). Speed limit 56 mph (90 kmph).

The speed limit in towns is 31 mph (50 kmph).

Toll Roads

These are first-rate, and have service stations approximately every 25 miles (40 km). The tolls are expensive, and are usually calculated according to distance traveled. You pay as you leave the toll road, but sometimes you receive a ticket when you enter that is to be handed in when you leave, to calculate what you owe. As you approach the *peaje* (toll booth), you will be confronted with several lanes. The *Telepago* lane is for cars that are fitted with a special chip on the windshield. The *Automatico* lane is for paying by credit card or the exact change. The *Manual* has an attendant who collects your fee. The lanes to use will display a green arrow (don't use one showing a red cross).

Parking

As a general rule, you may not park where the pavement is painted yellow, or, obviously, where a "no parking" sign is displayed. In major cities it is difficult to find free parking. There are parking spaces marked in blue, where you can usually leave the car for up to two hours, and will have to purchase a ticket from a machine or an attendant. Where possible, look for underground parking with security. It can be worth paying more.

You will note, however, that the Spanish pull in wherever they like, even stopping on crossings and pavements. Again, do not follow suit.

Penalties for parking infringements vary from town to town. If you park illegally, especially in a foreign car, you will almost certainly become a victim of the *grua*, the local tow truck. Getting your car back is a hassle, and expensive.

RULES OF THE ROAD

- Drive on the right. Give way to traffic from the right, especially at traffic circles.

- Do not turn left if there is a solid line along the middle of the road. This is a major cause of accidents on fast roads. There will be a special lane on the right, signed *Cambio de sentido*, which will take you on to a side road, and will then cross back over the main road.

- Traffic lights are not always located on the streets. They are sometimes suspended high in the air above the traffic, and can be hard to see in the sun. If you sit at a green light for more than a second, expect hooting from behind you.

- Watch out on pedestrian crossings— especially if you are the pedestrian—as they do not give you the right of way. Always be very careful before stepping out. Cars may not even slow down.

- Flashing headlights can mean anything from "the police are ahead" (if coming toward you) to "get out of my way, you're driving too slowly" (from behind). Like the horn, they are overused.

- You may notice car stickers with letters and flags. These will refer to the region they are from, and even abroad they are more numerous than the "E" (*España*) sticker.

- In keeping with their temperament, the Spanish often bend the rules a little. Don't be surprised when turn signals are not used—people stop wherever they wish, and speed limits are ignored. Do not follow suit.

TRAINS

Mainline Trains

RENFE (*Red Nacional de Ferrocarriles Españoles*), the national network of Spanish railways, runs most of the nearly 9,500 miles (approx. 15,000 km) of railway in Spain with fares that are among the cheapest in Europe. However, many of the trains are slow and uncomfortable, and do not have air-conditioning. For long journeys the TALGO (*Tren Articulado Ligero Goikoetxea Oriol*, a light articulated train), is a good option that is fast, comfortable, and efficient. TALGO and intercity trains have buffet and bar services on board, although the quality is indifferent and prices are high. AVE (*Alta Velocidad España,* "Spanish high velocity"—*ave* also means "bird"), fast trains between Madrid and Seville, and Madrid and Málaga, were introduced in 1992. You can now get from Madrid to Málaga in just over four hours instead of seven, and to Seville in only two and a half hours.

The better the train, the more expensive the ticket. Check the various options available, as there are discounts for frequent travelers and students. There are information desks at all the big stations. You can also book seats with authorized travel agents, who will charge a small commission but will usually be more helpful and relaxed. Always book a seat on long journeys.

Narrow-Gauge Trains
There are other railway companies in Spain in charge of the narrow-gauge tracks that still serve parts of the country, especially in the north. Some of the trains are used only by tourists, while others are a normal way of local travel. One example is the narrow-gauge line that runs from Alicante to Denia on the Costa Blanca. Built in 1914 to transport fresh produce to Alicante, the fifty-seven-mile (ninety-three-kilometer) route passes

colorful fishermen's houses, deep gorges, and the whitewashed village of Altea.

Other tourist options are available. Some steam trains have been restored and brought back into use. One is the *Tren de la Fresa* (Strawberry Train) running from Madrid to the palace at Aranjuez, so called because the line was used to take fresh strawberries to the capital. The tradition is carried on to this day, with fresh strawberries being handed out to passengers.

If you want to experience the ultimate train journey, take one of the country's luxurious specials, built in the 1920s. The *Transcantabrico* follows the north coast of Spain from San Sebastian to Santiago de Compostela on an eight-day trip. The four coaches include a bar with a resident disk jockey. At night the train parks in stations to allow passengers to get a good night's sleep.

In the south the *Al Andalus Express* is a mobile hotel consisting of twelve coaches, which follows a route taking in all the Moorish sites of Andalusia. There are two luxury restaurants, a bar, a lounge, and a games car.

INTERURBAN BUSES

Throughout Spain there are many good private companies with coaches that are well maintained and offer cheap travel. They often take a more direct route than the trains. Most towns will have a bus terminal (*estación de autobus*). You can buy tickets here or from a travel agent, and should always book in advance, especially for weekends and holidays. Long journeys will usually have short refreshment stops, but be sure to get back to the bus punctually. They may not wait for those who are late.

URBAN TRANSPORT

Madrid and Barcelona have bus, metro, and local train networks servicing the cities. In both cities the metro is the fastest and most efficient way of moving around.

Metro (Underground Train Systems)

Madrid has eleven underground lines, identified by a number and color-coded on maps. The service operates from 6:00 a.m. to 1:30 a.m. Tickets can be bought at all stations, from machines or staffed ticket booths. For multiple journeys buy a *Metrobus* ticket, valid for ten trips on the Metro or buses.

The service in Barcelona is similar. It is open from 5:00 a.m. to midnight on Sunday to Thursday and from 5:00 a.m. to 2:00 a.m. on Friday, Saturday, and on the eve of local holidays. Tickets are available for single or multiple journeys. Tourist options include three-day and five-day tickets with unlimited journeys, or the airbus+bus+metro ticket that allows you to use the various types of transport for unlimited travel during your stay and includes a return ticket to the airport. Check the information desks for the various options.

Buses

Buses run daily from 6:30 a.m. to 11:30 p.m., and about every ten to fifteen minutes on most routes. There is also a night bus service after midnight called the *Buho* (owl) in Madrid and the *Nitbus* (nightbus) in Barcelona. Fewer buses run on Sundays and public holidays.

Bus stops have useful maps of the routes. Raise your arm to stop the bus. There is one standard fare for all journeys. The ticket can be bought once you are on the bus (many of the city buses only accept the correct change), or you can buy a *Metrobus* ticket (see opposite), valid for ten trips by bus or metro. These can also be purchased from bus information stands, *estancos* (tobacconists), and newsstands.

Web Sites

Some useful Web sites on the subject of transport appear in the Resources section on page 164.

Taxis

There is no shortage of taxis in Spain, and they are cheap. They are different colors in different cities, but all have a sign on the roof with a green light that comes on when the taxi is available. There are taxi stands, or you can just stop one in the street. They have meters, but extra is added at night, on weekends, and if you have luggage. If you are going on a long journey, ask and agree on the approximate price beforehand. As for tipping, people usually give 10 percent, or just round up the fare.

WHERE TO STAY

Tourism has brought a great deal of wealth to Spain, but it has also spoiled the Mediterranean coastline, where high-rise hotels and apartment complexes were thrown up without much thought for overall design in the 1960s and 1970s. There is no shortage of accommodation generally, either in these coastal resorts or inland. All large towns and cities have plenty of places to stay, ranging from luxurious hotels to cheap and cheerful *hostales*, and local tourist offices have lists of what is available. It is always worth making reservations in advance, especially if you are visiting a town during festival time.

Hotels

These conform to European standards, and range
from five stars down, according to the facilities
offered. They are of all shapes and sizes, and some
are traditional, others overtly modern.

One type of hotel peculiar to Spain is the
parador. These started as a group of historic
buildings converted into hotels by the
government in the 1920s, in part to
preserve them, but also to encourage
travel to less-visited parts of the
country. Today, there are eighty-five such
establishments spread throughout Spain. About
a third of them are historic buildings, while others
are tastefully designed new buildings constructed
in styles authentic to their regions, often in
picturesque villages or highly scenic locations.
The older buildings have all been restored, and all
have modern hotel facilities.

Hostales

These abound in all cities, and tourist offices will
give you a list. They are cheaper than hotels and also
have a "star" rating. They are often housed on two
floors of an apartment complex, with a reception
area, television room, dining room, and some
bedrooms on one floor, and the remainder of the
bedrooms on the floor above. *Hostales* are usually
family-run, and the staff may speak only Spanish.

Bedrooms will not always have their own bathrooms, and meals are not usually included. Breakfast may be available—usually coffee and a pastry—but most people prefer to go out to a nearby bar.

Albergues

These are youth hostels. They have dormitory-style rooms and a dining room and kitchen where you can cook for yourself. They are usually situated near major railway stations in the cities, or in some of the nature reserves scattered throughout Spain. They are cheap, basic, and populated mainly by young backpackers.

Apartamentos

These self-contained apartments can be rented in the coastal regions. They can be anything from rooms furnished with the basics to small *villas* with a garden area. Prices will depend on size, location, and the time of year. (Apartments for long-term residency are called *pisos*.)

Agroturismo

This is a new trend that is more popular in the Basque Country, where large houses in the country rent out rooms, than in the rest of Spain. It is an attempt to open up rural areas to tourism, both for the local people and for foreigners, and these rooms are a good idea for walking vacations, or just for getting away from the stress of city life.

HEALTH AND INSURANCE

Pharmacists can usually deal with minor health problems, and even medication that in other countries may need a prescription, such as antibiotics, can often be sold over the counter.

Spain has a very good national health service that works alongside an excellent private sector. Hospitals are of a very high standard.

Private travel insurance for all visitors is highly recommended. Nationals of EU countries, however, are entitled to free medical treatment in Spain. The relevant forms must be obtained before leaving your country of origin. For example, form E111, for the British, is available from post offices.

chapter eight

BUSINESS BRIEFING

People coming to Spain to do business are struck by three things: the cultural differences between the regions, the need for a continuing relationship for successful business, and the fact that the Spaniards leave things until the last minute.

Spain is divided into eighteen autonomous regions. The most important business areas are Madrid and the center, Barcelona and its surrounding area, and Andalusia in the south. People from Barcelona and its region, Catalonia, have a totally different attitude to work from the people of any other part of Spain. They can come across as direct, even abrupt, and are less expressive than their fellow countrymen. Other Spaniards consider them to be hardworking, frugal, aloof, and humorless. The Catalans find the Madrileños, the people from Madrid, arrogant, bureaucratic, and extravagant tricksters who like showing off. The Andalusians are even more laid-back, more prone to long lunch breaks and to doing business outside the office. Their attitude to timetables and appointments—very relaxed—is the total opposite of the Catalans'.

What is common to all, however, is the fact that, as in Italy and Portugal, good personal relations are the *sine qua non* of successful business. With good personal relations, a business may still fail, but without them there will be no business at all. Deadlines may not be adhered to unless contact is maintained. The personal relationship gives importance to the matter at hand, and deliveries will be ready if you follow them up.

COMPANY ORGANIZATION AND BEHAVIOR

Spain has two forms of company, the stock company, *Sociedad Anónima* (SA), and the limited company, *Sociedad de Responsibilidad Limitada* (SRL). Companies with more than fifty employees must have a works committee. Companies with more than five hundred employees have an employee representative on the board.

Offices tend to work a forty-hour week, from 9:00 a.m. to 1:00 or 2:00 p.m., with two hours or more for lunch, and then from 3:00 p.m. to 6:00 or 7:00 p.m. or even later. These hours may be adjusted in the south to allow for a longer lunch break. Deals are often agreed upon in principle over lunch or dinner, with subordinates fleshing out the details with you later, in the office.

People may take a four-day weekend over public holidays. In July and August, most people go away on vacation, and the offices may change their working hours, have only a skeleton staff, or often, in August, close down altogether.

Leadership and Hierarchy
The Spanish management style is "top down," with all key decisions being made by the boss. This is typical of the older-established companies and family firms, where the president is the absolute controller and subordinate positions are held by members of the family. Knowledge of English is not automatic among older managers, who may speak French as their first business language. You should check whether you will need an interpreter. Quite often the managing director or chairman will have a younger manager who will translate. Spain does have a professionally trained cadre of managers, many of whom have studied in the U.S.A., are up-to-date on modern management techniques, and speak excellent English.

A Spanish boss (*jefe*) is expected to make decisions and to be courageous. He (and it usually is a he) is also expected to work at gaining and maintaining the personal loyalty of his subordinates. His decisions will be concise, concrete, and short-term, with clear instructions as to how to implement them. However, managers may not feel committed to implementing them, and will pass even small decisions back up the line. This is especially true in the civil service, where immense bureaucracy can slow things down. Written objectives and profiles are unusual, as are appraisals.

Spanish managers work less from logic than from intuition, and they pride themselves on their personal influence with their staff. A Spanish manager is expected to be aware not only of the business lives but also of the personal lives of the staff, and to be prepared to deal with problems in either area. Instructions are never given coldly. Warmth is an important part of giving orders and instructions, especially in the south, but the underlying authority is always clear. Logic is secondary to force of emotion.

Human Responsiveness
If a Spanish employee approaches his or her boss with a personal problem, it is important to pay attention to it immediately, even if only to make an appointment to deal with it or discuss it in more detail later. The personal and human dimension takes priority.

The Spanish executive generally likes to work near his or her family. A few years may be spent studying and working in Madrid, but then employment is usually sought in the hometown. In many companies connections (*enchufe*), rather than qualifications or aptitude, are still the key to recruitment. Education is still regarded as extremely important, but other qualities are expected as part of the package. The qualifications for promotion are personal loyalty, friendship, and ability, in that order. Intelligence alone may seem a bit suspect.

BUSINESS STYLE

Although Spain is a hot country, appearance is important, and people are expected to dress in an acceptably businesslike and stylish fashion—dark suits or navy blue blazers and ties for men, and formal suits or dresses, always with nylons, for women. Jackets and ties may be removed in the office. Symbols of wealth in clothes, watches, cars, and jewelry show that you have done well. The Spaniards take great pride in their possessions, and set store by quality and taste. Your Mont Blanc pen or Cartier watch will be quietly noticed and appreciated, but not commented upon.

Spanish business style is generally quite informal and relaxed, but first meetings are formal. A senior man, for example the president of a company, named Don Sr. José Antonio López, might be addressed as Don José Antonio or Don José. Use the formal *Usted*, and change to the informal *tú* only if suggested by your hosts. You will probably move to first-name terms rapidly, and continue in this informal style thereafter.

It is important to have a relationship based on trust. It is also important not to be overassertive, as this may impinge on personal pride. The Spaniards take more pride in their personal qualities, in particular personal honor, than in their business or technical excellence. The personal touch is all-important, and getting out of the office to chat and "network" is part of the job. One cup of coffee with you may count for more than a hundred exchanges of e-mails. If you are in another country, then a telephone conversation can fulfill the same function.

At work, although there may be one lunchroom for all staff, Spanish colleagues tend to mix with people at the same level rather than with their seniors and juniors, even if they are on the same team. The bosses tend to have lunch with clients at a restaurant where they are well known.

WOMEN IN BUSINESS

Despite the traditional Spanish *macho* image, there are many women in middle and senior management positions, and their qualifications ensure that they are universally accepted. That said, however, you will not often meet a woman at the top of a Spanish company—unless she is the daughter or granddaughter of the founder.

Businesswomen expect a completely professional attitude from the men they are dealing with in business. A lunch or dinner invitation will be considered as part of the business relationship. Whoever extends the invitation, pays.

THE BUSINESS RELATIONSHIP

To do business in Spain you must first earn the trust of your Spanish counterpart by establishing a personal relationship. Your business partners will be hospitable, and any social invitation should be regarded as an investment in a trusting relationship. Talking about families and children is an important part of this, and having photos of your family ready to show will help greatly in building the relationship. It will demonstrate to your Spanish counterpart that you have roots in your society, and therefore a stake in ensuring that things are done correctly.

The social relationship extends to small family favors. If you can help a relative or friend of your business partner in some way, it will be seen as a real favor, and will be of immense value in building trust. A successful business relationship has to move beyond mere good business relations.

For a man in business, pride and the *macho* image are still important. Crucial to Spanish business is the concept of honor and of not losing dignity. Spanish business partners are men and women of their word. Once you have established a relationship, they will not let you down. By the same token, you must be careful not to do anything that lets them down in the eyes of their peers.

One key aspect of this is the employment of Spanish agents to act on your behalf. They are your eyes and ears in the market, and once you employ them you must work with them—they will be very unhappy if you make any move behind their back. Make sure you choose such contacts wisely, as they can make or break your presence in the Spanish market.

FLEXIBILITY

A Spanish businessperson, although equipped with agenda and timetables, also prides him or herself on being flexible. This often means that planning may seem more haphazard and projects may progress at a slower rate than you would expect or like. The Spaniards prefer long-term visions and short-term plans. They can do this because of the immense importance of networking in Spanish society. It has been maintained that they can achieve in three days what for an American or German might take three months, because they can do it all personally, on the telephone. Their years of networking mean that they can achieve things through personal contact that would be quite difficult for their U.S. or European counterparts.

The Spaniards know how to cram a lot in. This means that they are essentially multitasking, juggling a number of things and reacting to the most important or urgent requirement. Once again, your personal relationship may make *you* the most important personal requirement.

MAKING APPOINTMENTS

The Spaniards, like the British, write the day first, then the month, then the year, so November 15, 2003 is written 15.11.03. When making an appointment, book ahead, and then telephone and confirm it on arrival. When you arrive for an appointment, the most appropriate way to announce yourself is to present your business card to the receptionist, who will let your Spanish contact know that you have arrived. Although you should be punctual yourself, do not be annoyed or discouraged if you are kept waiting for fifteen or even thirty minutes.

Keep in mind the normal business working hours, and remember that hours are often reduced, or offices are closed altogether, in general holiday periods. Avoid scheduling appointments around Easter or Christmas.

COMMUNICATION STYLE

The Spanish business communication style is relaxed and friendly, and relies above all on the human touch. It is important when sending a business e-mail to a Spaniard to be slightly more long-winded and warm than you might be in a similar e-mail to a U.S.A. or U.K. contact. Always be warm and friendly, use "Dear" or "Hi" to begin with, and end with "Regards" or "Best regards." On the telephone also, do not forget the human side.

MEETINGS

In Spain, the traditional function of a meeting is either to get to know clients, or to communicate instructions. A meeting does not generally have an agenda, but flows as a conversation. Topics are raised and dropped as relevant to the point under discussion. The final decision will always remain with the boss, and if he or she cannot take part in the full discussion they will usually check in to make their presence known in the course of the discussion or negotiation.

The Spaniards will begin a meeting with a long speech that serves to establish their own status and qualifications as well as to outline their aims. This is followed by an equally long response from the other side. It is important during a meeting to find points of agreement to comment on wherever possible. Honor demands that a Spanish boss should not be contradicted in public, and a "compliant" foreigner may well gain concessions in a more relaxed atmosphere over lunch or dinner.

The meetings culture is not well established in Spain, and the idea of thrashing things out to arrive at a common agreement is not universally recognized, nor are action points or follow-ups. It is important for the person in the chair, however, to win everyone over to his or her point of view. The chairperson will either make the decisions or will have to put the decision made to the boss for ratification.

Spanish managers are quite individualistic, and will use a meeting to score personal points. They have an expressive style and negotiations can be loud, with frequent interruptions, and people called in at short notice to contribute to the negotiation. It is important not to be upset by conversational overlap, which is not felt to be rude in Spain. Negotiations (often lengthy) depend on intuition and thinking on your feet rather than the careful preparation of, say, German and Swiss companies. The personal touch is enhanced by strong eye contact. Spaniards want to be able to "read your eyes," to know who you are, and may be quite delicate about saying "no."

PRESENTATIONS

The Spaniards, who are not always dedicated listeners, and who read perhaps the least in Europe, may be less concerned with content than with style and appearance. They will observe your physical characteristics, your mannerisms, and your willingness to participate in the congenial socializing that will follow. If you are making a "substance" presentation, keep it short, and use a few imaginative phrases that people will remember. The Spaniards will want to interject and discuss what you say, so a thirty-minute presentation should be the limit.

PLANNING AND CONTROL

The dependence on the personal relationship means that standard company functions, such as strategic planning, and even financial business plans, may be based on business sense and intuition rather than on systematic data. Schedules, budgets, and forecasts will be rough guides only, and delivery dates should not be taken literally. Everything must be done by personal negotiation. It is no good waiting for the deadline to pass and then calling up to check why stock has not been delivered. "Inspect, not expect," should be your motto.

A Spanish representative, working in Spain for a London-based British company, had for some months been underperforming in the market. An executive of the British company flew over to visit the offices in an attempt to find out what had gone wrong. He talked to each staff member personally, then took them all out to lunch, and generally formed a good relationship with them. "Now that we feel we know you," said some of the staff, as he left, "we'll try to do better for your products." And they did. Sales rose 50 percent.

BUSINESS ENTERTAINING

Be prepared to spend some time outside the office on building and maintaining good relations. Although today's business world no longer always allows for a *siesta* in the afternoon, the Spaniards still start work early and finish late, going out to dinner as late as 10:00 p.m. and finishing at 2:00 a.m. Weekend socializing can go on far later. Be prepared for the strain on your constitution—and on your digestion!

Business entertaining usually takes place in restaurants. If you are invited to a Spanish home, it may just be for a drink before moving on to dinner in a restaurant. You may otherwise be taken first for *tapas* in a café or bar.

Spanish business protocol dictates that you wait until coffee is served at the end of the meal before bringing up the subject of business.

Whoever has extended the invitation pays the bill. If you have been invited out for a meal, you should return the compliment at a later date, but when doing so you should be careful not to mention "repaying" your hosts. When the time comes to choose a restaurant, ensure that it is an excellent one, as the Spaniards are extremely appreciative of fine food and wine, and will respect you for your good taste! Do not forget that many restaurants close for a month of vacation.

GIFT GIVING

Gifts are not usually given at a first meeting, but may serve as a sign of willingness to establish the relationship at a later date. They may also be given at the conclusion of successful negotiations. If you receive a gift, you should open it immediately. A small case of local wine or produce is a typical gift.

If you are taking gifts, do not give anything too extravagant, or your generosity may be perceived as a bribe. Presents of single malt whiskey, good English gin, or chocolates are very acceptable. If you want to give a bottle of Spanish wine, make sure that it is a special one, such as Vega Sicilia. Your country's local crafts, illustrated books, tapes, and CDs related to your home region are also often appreciated. Only give a gift advertising your company name if it is discreet and tasteful.

On the rare occasion that you might be invited for a meal at a Spanish home, take a box of good chocolates, or dessert items such as attractive little pastries, or flowers—but count these, for thirteen flowers are always considered bad luck. Be sure to avoid buying dahlias or chrysanthemums, as these flowers are associated with death.

CONCLUSION

In business, as in most areas of Spanish life, the importance of personal relationships must not be underestimated. At first there is formality, but once introductions are over a more personal, informal approach is expected. However, dignity must always be maintained, and respect and honor are necessary for building trust and a working relationship.

Spanish business is "multitasking"—many things are dealt with at the same time, not separately. You, too, will be expected to be flexible. You should prioritize a good working relationship with both colleagues and subordinates. Good contacts are crucial as the concept of *enchufe* (the right contact) is a part of business life. If you are well considered by the right people, you are on your way toward success. Your product will be more easily accepted once your business partners accept you and like you.

Looking to the future, the new, professionally trained managers will have a new approach. Their training in a more decentralized, team-based, target-oriented, and quality-focused management will become the norm in Spanish business as the older *patrones* retire.

chapter nine

COMMUNICATING

LANGUAGE

Spanish is the official language of Spain and of
many other countries: Argentina, Bolivia, Chile,
Colombia, Costa Rica, Cuba, the Dominican
Republic, Ecuador, El Salvador, Equatorial Guinea,
Guatemala, Honduras, Mexico, Nicaragua,
Panama, Paraguay, Peru, Uruguay, and Venezuela.
It is also the official language of the commonwealth
of Puerto Rico, and is widely spoken in several
other nations, including the United States of
America, Morocco, and the Philippines.

Spanish and English vie for the position of the
world's second most-spoken language after
Chinese (885 million). In 1999, Spanish had 332
million speakers, while English had 322 million.
When people who speak English as a second
language are included, however, the positions are
reversed.

Castilian (*Castellano*)

Although generally known as Spanish, the correct
name for Spain's official language is Castilian. It

began as a dialect spoken in northern Spain, but became the language of the court of the kingdom of Castile and León in the twelfth century. When Isabella and Ferdinand united their kingdoms of Castile and Aragon, it became the official language of the state. Like other European languages it stems from Latin, but has also adopted words from other languages, including many Arabic words from the time of Moorish dominance.

There are differences in accent and, to a lesser extent, in vocabulary, in Castilian in various regions of the country. The most significant difference is in the pronunciation of the letter combinations "*ce*," "*ze*," and "*za*." In northern Castile, where the language is said to be spoken in its purest form, this is pronounced as a soft English "th"; in southern and western Spain it is pronounced as an English "s." The "s" pronunciation is also found in Latin American Spanish. There is no snobbery about accents in Spanish. Your accent tells the listener which area you come from, not which class you belong to.

Castilian is the country's most widely spoken language, although nearly 30 percent of the population have a different first language. These languages include Catalan (12 percent of the population), Galician (8 percent) and Basque (just over 1 percent). The constitution of 1978 gave the dominant regional languages and dialects official status, along with Castilian. Those stipulated are Catalan in Catalonia and in the Balearic Islands; Valencian in Valencia; *Euskera* (Basque) in the Basque Country and in the territory of Navarre; Aragonese in Aragon; and *Gallego* (Galician) in Galicia. *Bable* (spoken in Asturias) and Aranese, spoken in the Aran Valley (Catalonia) are other languages that are protected, although they do not have co-official status. All of these languages except *Euskera* (Basque) are Romance languages that evolved from Latin. *Euskera* is a "language isolate," totally unrelated to any other language. Many of these languages are taught regularly in school and used in radio and television broadcasts within their regions.

Spain's tradition of regionalism has been a major factor in recognizing the various languages. Other countries in Europe have several local languages, but few of these have official recognition. For the foreigner in Spain this will not cause any difficulties. Castilian is spoken and understood everywhere, although in some areas people will not be as fluent in it as in their local language. However, if you learn a few words of any local language people will appreciate your efforts.

Catalan
Catalan is closely related to Provençal, a language spoken in southern France, and is spoken by the

majority of the population in Catalonia, Valencia, and the Balearic Islands. There are differences in the way Catalan is spoken in these three regions, and in the 1980s there were politically motivated disputes as to whether Valencian was a Catalan dialect or a distinct language. It has a long and distinguished history as a literary language. It flourished especially during the Middle Ages but declined after the fifteenth century. A revival known as the Renaixença (Renaissance), which began in the mid-nineteenth century, renewed interest in the language leading to the Pompeu Fabra grammar, the basis of Catalan as it is taught today.

Galician (*Gallego*)

This is spoken in Galicia, in the northwestern corner of Spain, and is the ancestor of modern Portuguese. It was the language of courtly literature until the fourteenth century, when it was displaced by Castilian. From then until the late nineteenth century, when there was a literary revival, its use was limited to everyday speech, and it was more common among country people than in the cities. In neighboring Asturias, the ancient local language of *Bable* is still spoken.

Basque (*Euskera*)

This is the most distinctive of the languages spoken in Spain. Neither a Romance nor an Indo-

European language, it predates the arrival of the Romans in Spain. Until the end of the nineteenth century Basque was spoken mostly in the countryside, and it had no significant literary tradition. In the twentieth century, and especially since it was made the official language of the Basque Country (*Euskadi*) in 1978, it has been used in all forms of writing.

Opposite are a few phrases in the various languages to get you started. You will notice that questions and exclamations in written forms are indicated by an inverted question mark (¿) or exclamation mark (¡) at the beginning of the sentence, and then a standard one at the end of the sentence. This avoids confusion between questions or exclamations and statements, which in speech may differ only in the tone of voice used, and this cannot be seen when written.

SPEAKING SPANISH

Spanish is considered one of the easiest foreign languages to learn, yet some foreigners live in Spain for years and never learn it or any of the other languages spoken here. Especially on the *costas* (coasts) there are foreign communities that are almost self-sufficient, and the local people involved with them often learn to speak the dominant language (usually English or German).

SOME USEFUL PHRASES

ENGLISH	CASTILIAN	CATALAN	GALICIAN	BASQUE
Hello	Hola	Hola	Ola	Kaixo
Good morning	Buenos días	Bon dia	Bon dia	Egun on
Good afternoon	Buenas tardes	Bona tarda	Boa tarde	Arratsalde on
Good night	Buenas noches	Bona nit	Boa noite	Gabon
Good-bye	Adiós	Adéu	Adeus	Agur
Please	Por favor	Si us plau	Por favor	Mesedez
Thank you	Gracias	Gracies	Gracias	Eskerrik asko
Excuse me	Perdón	Perdona	Desculpa	Barkatu
Cheers!	¡Salud!	Salut!	Saude!	Topa!
Is there a hotel near here?	¿Hay un hotel por aquí?	Hi ha un hotel per aquí?	Hai algun hotel aquí perto?	Bal al da hotelik hemen inguruan?
Where is the bus station?	¿Donde está la estación de autobus?	On es l'estació d'autobus?	Onde está a estación de autobus?	Non dago autobus-geltokia?

However, if you have a basic knowledge of Spanish, and use it, this will show that you have an interest in the culture, and it will be greatly appreciated.

Spain is a great country for practicing the language. The basic grammar is straightforward, but in any case nobody worries if your Spanish is not grammatically correct, or if you make mistakes. In tourist areas the local people will probably be able to communicate in different languages, but away from there even stumbling Spanish will open up the possibility of communication. A gregarious people, the Spanish love talking, and will do their best to converse with you.

A phrase book translating basic phrases from your own language to Spanish and a pocket dictionary are probably all you need, to begin with. However, if you plan to stay for a while or will be visiting Spain often, consider doing a basic Spanish course. It will pay dividends.

Spanish Pronunciation

Written Spanish is almost completely phonetic. Once you know how to pronounce the letters and where to stress the words, you can make a good attempt at reading it. Here are the most basic rules:

The Spanish alphabet consists of twenty-eight letters: *a, b, c, ch, d, e, f, g, h, i, j, k, l, ll, m, n, ñ, o, p, q, r, s, t, u, v, x, y, z.*

The vowels, *a, e, i, o,* and *u* sound like the vowels in the English words "ha," "hay," "he," "ho," and "who."

The consonants *b* and *v* are pronounced very similarly to each other, as are *ll* and *y*. Spanish speakers also drop *h* sounds at the beginning of words, so that *horario* (schedule) and *historia* (history) are pronounced as if they were spelled *orario* and *istoria*. These three elements of the language account for the most common mistakes made by people learning Spanish as a second language: confusing *b* with *v*, pronouncing *ll* as though in English, and sounding the *h* at the beginning of words where it should be silent.

Most Spanish words ending with a vowel or the consonants *n* or *s* are pronounced with the stress on the penultimate syllable, for example, *vino, casa, abuela, viven, antes* (pronounced *bee*no, *kass*a, ab*way*la, *bee*ben, *an*tes, and meaning wine, house, grandmother, they live, before). Words ending in consonants other than *n* or *s*, however, are stressed on the last syllable, for example, *ciudad, feliz, municipal, hotel* (pronounced seeoo*dad*, fell*eeth*, moonithi*pal*, o*tel*, meaning city, happy, municipal, hotel). All words that are exceptions to these rules have an accent to show where the stress falls, for example, *estación, avión,* López (estathee*on*, meaning station, avi*on*, meaning airplane, and *Lo*peth, a surname).

FACE TO FACE

Whatever language you may be speaking, the Spanish have a typically Mediterranean manner. They stand quite close to the person they are speaking to, and will often touch the other person to emphasize a point. They gesticulate a lot, which can help the learner if the conversation is in Spanish, and they speak loudly. The combination of volume and forceful gestures often make it difficult to be sure whether two people are having a normal conversation or an argument!

In a formal situation the voices may be slightly lowered, gestures will be restrained, and the *Usted* form will be used. As we have seen, this is similar to the *vous* form in French, but is not used as frequently. It is a polite and respectful form of address that is reserved when speaking to older people, or perhaps to business associates in a formal meeting.

There are no taboo subjects, but to start with it is probably safer to stay with topics of general interest rather than to ask a somebody a lot of personal questions. Complimentary remarks and questions about the local area will always start the conversation going, and you will soon find points of common interest to discuss. As mentioned before, if the Spanish are talking negatively about themselves and their culture, you should be diplomatic and not join in.

SERVICES

Post
The postal service is quite good in Spain, although many people complain about it. The post office (*correos*) is open from 9:00 a.m. to 2:00 p.m. on Monday to Friday, and 9:00 a.m. to 1:00 p.m. on Saturday, but you can buy stamps from a tobacconist (*estanco*). Mailboxes are bright yellow. Sometimes there will be a separate one for letters going abroad (*al extranjero*).

The mail is delivered once a day. Small packages will be delivered to the house, but larger ones will be kept at the post office and will have to be collected. Do not forget to bring the notice they left you, and some form of identification.

Telephone
The national company, *Telefónica*, controls line rental, although it now has to compete with other companies over the prices of calls. You may use different companies for different types of calls. Every Spanish province has a different two- or three-figure prefix. Telephone numbers consist of nine digits, including the prefix. The national code is 34.

There are plenty of telephone booths (*cabinas*), and you can use coins, or cards purchased from a tobacconist, in them. Most of them have a facility for instructions in English, accessed by pressing the language button. The ringing tone is long, the busy tone shorter and rapid. It will cost you over sixty cents just to get through, and you will need a plentiful supply of coins. International and national calls are cheaper after 10:00 p.m. on weekdays, after 2:00 p.m. on Saturday, and all day Sunday.

The standard answer when answering the phone is "*Digame*," or "*Diga*," which mean "Speak to me," or "Speak."

Mobile telephones in Spain operate on the same principles as anywhere else in the world. There are predominantly pay-as-you-go phones, although all companies offer contracts whereby your call fees are deducted from your bank account on a monthly basis.

The Internet
There are Internet cafés in all the major cities and in most towns.

CONCLUSION
The Spanish are relaxed, sociable, and family-loving. Children are seen *and* heard at all times of the day and night. With the outdoor life of sunshine, crowds of people, good food and drink, and gossip, activity and good humor bustle

everywhere. You will probably very quickly get into the swing of it all, and will start to love the Spanish way of life.

As a business traveler, you might see some of the Spanish traits from a different angle. The lack of punctuality and the abhorrence of rules and regulations can be frustrating, and time seems to be measured differently in Spain. *Mañana* rules. But you are sure to find your Spanish contacts to be friendly and hospitable, and interested in you personally. Once they get to know you, you will be important to them, and your business is likely to flourish as a result.

Whatever your reason for going there, knowing more about the Spanish and their culture will help you to make the most of your time in Spain, and to have realistic expectations. Above all, it will help you to be at ease in a country where the individual is important and enjoying life is a priority.

¡Viva España!

Resources

There are plenty of Web sites giving useful information about Spain, and it is a good idea to consult them before you go. Here are a few to get you started.

www.uk.tourspain.es	Official Spanish National Tourist Office site.
www.tourspain.co.uk	Official Spanish National Tourist Office site.
www.tourspain.es	Official Spanish National Tourist Office site.
www.spaindata.com	General data on Spain.
www.okspain.com	Tourist information about all parts of Spain.
www.spainexpat.com	A Web page for expats living in Spain.
www.viamichelin.com	Detailed maps for all regions of Spain.
www.idealspain.com	Information on many sporting and leisure activities.

Transportation

Madrid	www.ctm-madrid.es
Barcelona	www.tmb.net
Renfe	www.renfe.es
Feve (northern Spain)	www.feve.es
Euskotren (Basque Country)	www.euskotren.es
FGV (Costa Blanca)	www.fgv.es
FGC (Catalunya)	www.fgc.es
Al Andalus Express	www.alandalusexpreso.com
Tren de la Fresa	www.ffe.es/delicias

Further Reading

Hooper, John. *The New Spaniards.* London: Penguin Books, 1995.

Carr, Raymond (ed.). *Spain: A History.* Oxford: Oxford University Press, 2000.

Zollo, Mike, with Phil Turk. *Spanish Language, Life, and Culture.* London: Teach Yourself Books, 2000.

Williams, Mark. *The Story of Spain: The Dramatic History of One of Europe's Most Fascinating Countries.* Málaga: Santana Books, 2000.

Tóibín, Colm. *Homage to Barcelona.* London: Simon and Schuster, 1990.

Franco, Silvana. *Great Tapas.* New York: Lorenz Books, 2000.

McGuiness, Victoria Miranda. *Simple Etiquette in Spain.* Folkestone, England: Simple Books, 1992.

Spanish. A Complete Course. New York: Living Language, 2005.

In-Flight Spanish. New York: Living Language, 2001.

Fodor's Spanish for Travelers (CD Package). New York: Living Language, 2005.

culture smart! spain

Index

culture smart! **spain**